9/98

18.⁹⁵

Historical American Biographies

SUSAN B. ANTHONY

Voice for Women's Voting Rights

Martha E. Kendall

Enslow Publishers, Inc.

44 Fadem Road   PO Box 38
Box 699   Aldershot
Springfield, NJ 07081 Hants GU12 6BP
USA   UK

Dedication:
This book is dedicated to the students and teachers at
Indian Landing School in Rochester, New York.

Library of Congress Cataloging-in-Publication Data

Kendall, Martha E., 1947-
    Susan B. Anthony : voice for women's voting rights / Martha E.
Kendall.
        p.   cm. — (Historical American biographies)
    Includes bibliographical references and index.
    Summary: Describes the life of the early women's rights activist who
fought for women's right to vote.
    ISBN 0-89490-780-8
        1. Anthony, Susan B. (Susan Brownell), 1820-1906—Juvenile
literature. 2. Feminists—United States—Biography—Juvenile literature.
3. Suffragists—United States—Biography—Juvenile literature.
[1. Anthony, Susan B. (Susan Brownell), 1820-1906. 2. Feminists.
3. Women—Biography.] I. Title. II. Series.
HQ1413.A55K45 1997
305.42'092—dc20
    [B]   96-30386
                                                        CIP
                                                         AC

Printed in the United States of America

10 9 8 7 6 5 4 3 2 1

Illustration Credits: Courtesy of Local History Division, Rochester
Public Library, Rochester, New York, pp. 65, 93; Courtesy of Special
Collections, Vassar College Libraries, pp. 39, 52; Courtesy of the Susan B.
Anthony House, Rochester, New York, p. 69; Courtesy of the author,
p. 114; Department of Rare Books and Special Collections, University
of Rochester Library, pp. 18, 19; Harpers New Monthly Magazine,
January 1852 p. 50; Library of Congress, pp. 55, 79, 94, 99, 105, 113;
Lucy Tilden Stewart Collection, Special Collections, University Library,
The University of Illinois at Chicago, p. 90; National Portrait Gallery,
p. 9; Photo courtesy of Ron and Lynn Ward, p. 109; The Schlesinger
Library, Radcliffe College, p. 101; Stephen Klimek, pp. 86, 111.

Cover Illustrations: *Ontario County Court House, Canadaigua, New
York,* © 1997 Charmaine Walters (background); Courtesy of Local
History Division, Rochester Public Library, Rochester, New York (inset).

CONTENTS

Acknowledgments

Many thanks to the following people who helped make failure impossible as I wrote this book: Linda Fuller; Ann Gordon; Colleen Hurst; Judy Bennett Jones; Amanda Morgan; Sally Roesch Wagner; and especially Lynn, Ron, and Michael Ward.

1

YOU'RE UNDER ARREST!

I have gone and done it!" boasted Susan B. Anthony.[1] She had voted in the election of 1872. But many people believed she had no reason to be proud. In fact, she was charged with a crime— "knowingly, wrongfully, and unlawfully voting."[2] Why was her voting "unlawful"? Because she was a woman! Susan B. Anthony claimed her gender should not make a difference, but Judge Ward Hunt did not see it that way.

The courtroom in Canandaigua, New York, was packed. People both for and against the idea of women voting crowded the audience. Even Millard Fillmore, a former president, came. The decision in

Susan B. Anthony's case was considered the test for whether any American woman would be allowed to vote.

The accused was a dignified, fifty-three-year-old woman. She wore her long, wavy hair pulled back into a neat bun. Although she stood only five feet five inches tall, the famous woman commanded respect. She was so well known that newspaper headlines did not need her last name. "Susan B." was enough. Writers often described her as selfless, generous, and determined.[3] She dedicated her life to winning women's right to vote, which she considered "the solution to everything."[4]

At the trial, her attorney, Henry Selden, defended her for over three hours. He claimed that Susan B. Anthony, just like any citizen of the United States, had the right to vote. He told the jury, "If the same act had been done by her brother . . ., the act would have been . . . honorable . . .; but having been done by a woman it is said to be a crime."[5]

The Judge's Verdict

Judge Hunt paid little attention to Selden. Hunt had already made up his mind about this case. He called the defendant "incompetent, as a woman, to speak for herself," and he refused to let her testify.[6] Then he read a statement he had prepared before the trial began. It said the Constitution guaranteed a general protection of citizens' rights, but those rights did not extend to women and voting. He directed the jury to find Susan B. Anthony guilty.

Angry and astonished, Selden objected. People on a jury are supposed to discuss a case among themselves, reach a decision, and then report their verdict to the judge. But Judge Hunt dismissed the jury before any member had a chance to speak. Selden protested that his client had not received a fair trial. He asked for a poll of the jury, a new trial, and an appeal. The judge said no.

Just before sentencing her, Judge Hunt asked if the defendant had anything to say. She certainly did! Several times Hunt tried to silence her, ordering her to sit down. But Susan B. Anthony stood firm. In a strong, clear voice, she said her rights had been trampled. "Robbed of the fundamental privilege of citizenship, I am degraded from the status of a citizen to that of a subject."[7]

She claimed that because of her unfair treatment in the trial, the judge could not legally sentence her. But the judge ordered her to pay a fine of one hundred dollars. She responded, "I shall never pay a dollar of your unjust penalty."[8] She pointed out that women had to pay taxes and they could be thrown in jail, fined, and hanged, but they were not allowed the basic right of voting. She concluded with a slogan from the American Revolution, "resistance to tyranny is obedience to God."[9]

Susan B. expected to be imprisoned for refusing to pay the fine. From jail she could appeal the decision to the Supreme Court. Judge Hunt knew that too. To prevent the case from going any further, he said she would not be imprisoned for failure to pay the fine.

The trial made national headlines. Some newspapers criticized Susan B. as being out to corrupt the law. The *Albany Law Journal* acknowledged that Judge Hunt had acted improperly, but then went on to say that "if Miss Anthony does not like our laws she'd better emigrate [leave the country]!"[10] Some newspapers emphasized Judge Hunt's behavior. The *Utica Observer* declared, "Such a case never before occurred in the history of our courts, and the hope is very general that it never will again. Justice Hunt outraged the rights of Susan B. Anthony."[11] The *N.Y. Daily Graphic's* front page showed a full-length drawing of her sporting an Uncle Sam hat. The caption read, "The Woman Who Dared."[12]

She was not the only person accused of a crime in connection with her voting. The inspectors who registered her were tried the next day. As a witness, Susan B. was asked, "'You presented yourself as a female, claiming you had a right to vote?' Quick as a

This formal portrait of Susan B. Anthony, taken in 1898, hangs in the National Portrait Gallery in Washington, D.C.

flash came her answer, 'I presented myself not as a female, sir, but as a citizen of the United States.'"[13] Repeating what he had done in Susan B.'s trial, Judge Hunt did not allow the jurors to vote and reach their own verdict. He ordered the jury to find the inspectors guilty. Each was charged twenty-five dollars, but two of them refused to pay. They went to jail. Susan B. asked some of her powerful political friends to request that President Ulysses S. Grant pardon the men, which he did. They were quietly released after five days.

Why would men be sent to jail for allowing Susan B. Anthony and her friends to register? How could voting be considered a crime?

The Crime of Voting

In the nineteenth century, many people opposed the idea of women voting. At that time, so-called proper women did not have any role in public society. Susan B. strongly disagreed with that attitude, especially when it came to voting. In 1872 she "decided to take matters into her own hands."[14]

Before voting, a citizen must register. Near Susan B.'s home in Rochester, New York, voters registered at a barber shop. On November 1, 1872, Susan B. led three of her sisters and twelve of her female friends to that barber shop in order to register for the upcoming election. The startled officials said the women could not. Susan B. read them the section of the Fourteenth Amendment to the United States Constitution that she believed gave all citizens the right to vote. She also read part of the New York State Constitution, which made no mention of maleness as a requirement for voting. The officials again said no. Then she said, "If you still refuse us our rights as citizens, I will bring charges against you in Criminal Court and I will sue each of you personally for large, exemplary damages!"[15] The inspectors discussed the situation and finally let her and the others register.

That afternoon, some Rochester newspapers urged the arrest of the inspectors who registered the women. Susan B. hurried back to their office. She promised them that she would cover any legal costs they might have to pay if they were fined. She did not want them to suffer for having done what she firmly believed to be the right thing.

Four days later, on November 5, Susan B. and the other women entered the polls. They voted early in the morning "so as to avoid the scene that would inevitably result from the spectacle of women voting."[16]

Newspapers quickly picked up the story. *The New York Times* said Susan B.'s bold act "should earn her a place in history."[17] The *Chicago Tribune* went so far as to say that "she would make as good a candidate for public office as she would a voter."[18] But she was not about to become a candidate; she was about to become a criminal.

Thirteen days after the election, deputy United States Marshal E. J. Keeney knocked on Anthony's door. He had not come for dinner. He was there to make a highly unusual arrest. Nervously dangling in his gloved hands a well-brushed high hat, the marshal acted embarrassed in the presence of the famous woman. Blushing, he stammered, "The commissioner wishes to arrest you."[19]

Susan B. did not expect to be arrested. She thought it more likely that she would have to defend the inspectors if they were charged a fine for registering her. But during many years of lecturing in favor of women's rights, she had learned how to handle the unexpected. Marshal Keeney seemed more uncomfortable than she did. He suggested that rather than his taking her to the commissioner, she could go alone whenever she was ready. Susan B. said she would not go voluntarily. She extended her wrists and said he must handcuff her and take her. The marshal refused to handcuff her. Instead, he simply accompanied her on the trolley to the commissioner's office. When the trolley conductor asked for her fare, she said loudly so everyone could hear, "I am traveling at the expense of the government. Ask him for my fare."[20]

Bail for her and the other women who had voted was set at five hundred dollars apiece. After paying bail, they would be free to leave until their trial. If they did not pay bail, they would wait for their trial in jail. All but Susan B. paid. She said the government had no right to imprison her, because she believed that she had not committed a crime. In response to her protest, the judge increased her bail to one thousand dollars.

She hoped that her case would eventually be heard by the United States Supreme Court. But Henry Selden, her attorney, paid her bail. His doing so implied she was not challenging the lawfulness of her arrest. She asked him, "Did you not know that you stopped me from carrying my case to the Supreme Court?"[21] He answered that he knew, but he could not allow a woman he respected to go to jail.

Susan B. could not change what Selden had done, so she made the most of her freedom to speak and travel before the trial began. She gave many speeches in the Rochester area, asking, "Is It a Crime for A Citizen of the United States to Vote?"[22] She addressed each audience as "Friends and *Fellow-Citizens.*"[23] Sometimes she stamped her right foot for emphasis. "It is downright mockery to talk to women of their enjoyment of the blessings of liberty while they are denied the only means of

Rights and Wrongs
Susan B. described her speeches in New York State as "talking to the people all about Woman's Rights, which means woman's wrongs, you know."[24]

securing them—the ballot."[25] Susan B. explained that "by voting in good faith, since she considered herself legally entitled to do so, she could not be held guilty of criminal action or intent."[26]

District Attorney Crowley's job was to prove Susan B.'s guilt. The accused was famous for being an excellent speaker. Crowley grew nervous because so many people in Rochester were listening to her.[27] She could be influencing men who might be the jurors in her trial. (Women were not allowed to serve on juries.) In May of 1873 he decided to move the trial out of Rochester to the small town of Canandaigua in neighboring Ontario County. The date was set for June 17, 1873. Susan B. immediately toured as much of that county as she could in the three weeks before the trial. Her friend Matilda Joslyn Gage spoke for her, too. Gage argued that it was "The United States on Trial, Not Susan B. Anthony."[28]

As far as Susan B. was concerned, the conclusion

of her trial showed only one person to be guilty: Judge Hunt. She believed that he had not ruled justly. But she hoped that a case in St. Louis, Missouri, that was tried about the same time as her own might produce the results she wanted. Virginia Minor sued an election inspector who refused to let her register. That case went to the Supreme Court. In 1874, the court ruled that the states had the power to give or deny voting rights. Just as states could rule that children and criminals could not vote, they could do the same regarding women. The Court said that the Fourteenth and Fifteenth Amendments to the United States Constitution forbade discrimination based on race but not sex.

Susan B. realized that the Constitution had to be changed before women could vote. A great deal of work lay ahead, and she was up to the challenge.

2

QUAKER CHILDHOOD

Challenges were nothing new to members of the Anthony family. Even before Susan was born, her parents had challenged their families' religious traditions.

Susan's parents, Daniel Anthony and Lucy Read, grew up on neighboring farms in Adams, Massachusetts. As playmates, they paid little attention to differences in their religions. Lucy's family were Baptists, but Daniel's were members of the Society of Friends, also known as Quakers.

Daniel left Adams in 1812 to study and then teach at the highly regarded Quakers' Nine Partners Boarding School in Dutchess County, New York. At age twenty-one he returned to Adams and set up a school at his parents' farm. Like other members of the community, the Reads wanted their children to benefit from the teaching of a person from the famous Nine Partners School. Lucy Read, the same age as her teacher, quickly became more than his student. She became his sweetheart.

Daniel Anthony loved this lively, blue-eyed young woman. She sang, danced, and wore fashionable clothes. He proposed to her, even though Quakers were not supposed to marry members of other religions. Daniel Anthony had no way of knowing that many years later he would have a daughter who was much like himself—following her own heart and mind, even if that meant challenging strong traditions.

Lucy Read understood that marrying a Quaker would put an end to her playful, light-hearted ways. Quakers believed in a plain lifestyle. They wore simple, drab clothing, and they did not dance or play music, cards, or games. Lucy Read loved Daniel Anthony, but she wanted one last dancing party before she married him and assumed the Quaker way of life. At the party, her future husband leaned against the wall and watched her dance with one partner after another until four o'clock in the morning.

When they became husband and wife on July 13,

1817, they also became the subject of much debate in Adams. People wondered how the Quakers would punish Daniel Anthony for his marriage to a non-Quaker.

Quaker leaders came to the home of Lucy Anthony's parents, the Reads. The newlyweds were living there while Daniel Anthony finished building their own home on the Savoy Road. Young Mrs. Anthony waited nervously in the parlor while the Quakers recited their verdict to her husband. They told him he was to be excluded from participating in any Quaker functions until he could "make satisfaction" (make up for his misbehavior) to the Society.[1]

At the end of the summer, he satisfied the

Quakers by writing this apology: "I am sorry that in order to marry the woman I love best, I had to violate a rule of the religious society I revered the most."[2] Lucy Anthony later said his letter showed that he "was sorry he

Susan B.'s father, Daniel Anthony.

married her," but it is more likely that if anyone had regrets about the marriage, it was she.[3] Even though she never became a Quaker, in accordance with their strict and somber ways, she gave up her stylish clothing and all her singing. As Mrs. Anthony, she assumed the quiet, supportive role of a hard-working and serious wife.

Susan's Early Years

Lucy Read Anthony gave birth to eight children, six of whom survived. Susan Brownell Anthony was the second child, born February 15, 1820. She was named after her father's sister, Susan Anthony Brownell. For her first six years, Susan's family lived in the house her father built. From its front yard, Susan could see the town of Adams, nestled about a mile away in the valley of the Hoosic River. Behind the house, looming in the dis-tance, stood Mount Greylock, the highest peak in Massachusetts.

Susan B.'s mother, Lucy Read Anthony.

Raised in the Quaker fashion, Susan and her sisters and brothers were not allowed toys, music, or games. Instead, Daniel Anthony wanted his children to learn self-discipline and conscientious ways. They still managed to have fun. Susan played the most with her sisters Guelma, one and a half years older, and Hannah, one and a half years younger. After finishing their chores, they romped in the snow during the long New England winters. When they got cold, the girls retreated to the attic where they made up stories to their hearts' delight.

The children also loved to visit their grandparents. At the Reads', Susan and her sisters gathered "like bees" around the tub of maple syrup kept in a small closet under the parlor stairs.[4] While the grownups talked, the girls feasted on the sweet syrup. Everything tasted good at their grandmother's: sweet cider, apples, doughnuts, and pudding.

When Susan was four, she and her older sister Guelma stayed with their Anthony grandparents for six weeks before the birth of baby Daniel. During the visit, Susan and Guelma learned how to read. Susan said, "We just loved those books and we pored over them."[5]

The girls returned home after Daniel was born. Their mother was shocked to see a change in Susan. Her eyes were crossed. Susan later wrote, "Mother was awfully distressed about it. She thought I had the prettiest eyes of any child she ever saw."[6] Believing that the hours of reading had strained the youngster's vision, Lucy Anthony put Susan's books away. After a few weeks, one of her eyes did straighten, but the other never recovered completely.

To support the family, Daniel Anthony farmed the land and ran a small general store. He also built a cotton mill, the first in Adams. The family prospered. As was common in those days, mill workers lived at the home of the mill owner. Lucy Anthony cooked, cleaned, sewed, washed, and ironed for her own family, as well as for the mill workers, sometimes numbering more than twelve at a time. The work seemed unending. Baking bread, "usually twenty loaves at a time, consumed an entire day."[7] Susan and the other children helped wash, iron, make clothes, and cook.

Battenville, New York

In 1826, John McLean of Battenville, New York, contacted Daniel Anthony. McLean had started a cotton manufacturing company. He had heard about Anthony's reputation for business success, and McLean suggested they work together to enlarge the factory. Daniel Anthony accepted the proposal. When Susan was six, the Anthony family moved to

Battenville, a tiny village in the Adirondack Mountains, forty miles west of Adams.

Battenville prospered largely due to the success of the cotton factory. Susan's father also established a machine shop and a general store. The store followed an unusual policy.

Most storekeepers offered their customers a drink of rum to conclude a business transaction. Daniel Anthony did not. Like most Quakers, he opposed the drinking of alcohol. He had seen many women and children abused by drunken husbands, and he did not want to add to the problem. McLean warned Anthony that if he had no rum in the store, no one would do business with him. Anthony replied, "Well, then, I'll close the store."[8] McLean did not have to worry. The store succeeded due to the high-quality merchandise offered at reasonable prices.

Normally the Quakers wore simple dark clothing, but one day Lucy Anthony presented Susan with a bright Scotch-plaid coat. Thrilled, Susan found excuses to admire herself in the mirror whenever possible. But her enjoyment of the coat did not last long.

One cold day she wore it when she accompanied her father to a Quaker meeting. She sat quietly by the stove during the proceedings, but a church member spotted her. Because Susan was not yet an official member, she was asked to leave. Instead of standing outside in the freezing cold, ten-year-old Susan walked to a neighbor's house. At their gate, a fierce dog jumped on her and ripped a big hole in the coat.

Not long afterward, all the Anthony children were accepted into the church. As Susan put it, they would never again be "turned out into the sleet and snow."[9]

Susan attended the one-room schoolhouse in Battenville. However, her natural delight in learning turned to frustration. Susan complained to her father that the teacher refused to show her how to do long division, perhaps because he did not know how to do it himself or simply "because she was a girl."[10] Anthony decided to start a home school for his children, which he would open in the evening to the mill workers and their children, too.

Although no university in America admitted women at the time, Daniel Anthony sought the best educated young woman available to teach at his school. Mary Perkins was his choice. Her advanced notions prompted her to set up a modern school that "was the first in that neighborhood to have a separate seat for each pupil, and although only a stool without a back, it was a vast improvement on the long bench running around the wall, the same height for big and little."[11] Mary Perkins taught the children to recite poems, she showed them picture books, and she led them in physical exercise. Many people believed that girls should not study too hard, for if they overworked their minds, their bodies would suffer. As a result, it was said, they might have trouble bearing children. In Mary Perkins's modern school, girls and boys exercised both their minds and bodies.

From the example of the mill workers and Mary Perkins, Susan and her sisters saw that young women could earn their own money. When a spooler at the mill was sick, both Susan and her younger sister Hannah begged their father to let them substitute for her. He decided they could draw straws to see who would work, and the winner would split the three-dollar wages with the loser. Susan won. She worked for two weeks. With her share of the money, Hannah bought a green beaded bag. Susan used hers to buy her mother six blue china cups.

During her two weeks in the mill, Susan worked under the watchful eye of Sally Ann Hyatt, one of the most experienced mill girls. Later, Anthony appointed a male supervisor to watch over Sally Ann. Susan asked, "Since Sally Ann knows much more about weaving and the machinery than he does, why didn't you appoint her supervisor instead?"[12] Susan's father did not dispute Sally

Ann's superior skill. Instead, he said that men always had supervising positions, and "It would never do to have a woman overseer in the mill."[13] Although the Quakers claimed to believe in the equality of the sexes, even Susan's progressive father continued the tradition of male bosses at work.

One career for women that was growing in respectability was teaching. Although female teachers earned much less than male teachers, they could earn enough money to have a better life than most nurses, farm help, factory workers, mill girls, or maids, the only other jobs open to females. When Susan was fifteen, she began teaching at her father's school during the summer. She taught the youngest children while the older students helped on their family farms.

An Education at Miss Moulson's

In 1837, a serious economic depression hit the country. The national banking system fell apart, and business owners like Daniel Anthony found themselves on the edge of bankruptcy. At the time, Susan's older sister Guelma was attending a new Quaker boarding school, Deborah Moulson's Female Seminary, in Hamilton, Pennsylvania. Guelma managed to remain at the school by securing a position as a teaching assistant. The Anthony family struggled to scrape up the tuition fee of $125 for Susan to attend the school as well.

In November, Susan's father took her to Hamilton. The trip marked the biggest adventure of Susan's young and sheltered life. She and her father set out during a snowstorm, traveling in an open wagon pulled by the family's horse. In Albany, New York, they boarded a steamboat for New York City. After riding in other boats and carriages, they concluded their one-week journey on foot, walking from a carriage stop to the seminary. Susan could hardly bear to see her father leave, writing in her diary, "It seemed impossible for me to part with him."[14] Susan felt as homesick as if she were on the other side of the earth.

The school's strict headmistress, Deborah Moulson, added to Susan's unhappiness. Harsh and critical of the students, Miss Moulson scolded Susan because on one of her compositions she had not dotted the i's properly. Susan's feelings were badly hurt. She wrote in her diary, "I do consider myself such a bad creature that I cannot see any who seems worse."[15]

When Deborah Moulson faulted the girls for failing to keep the school clean, Susan resolved to clean a classroom herself. She was determined to do a good job. One day, in order to reach the cobwebs on the high ceiling, she stood on Miss Moulson's desk. But then to her horror, the latch on the top of the desk broke. Susan confessed, but Miss Moulson pretended not to hear her. She then asked other girls to identify the guilty person. Susan had to listen in silence as they named her. Her eyes brimming, it was all she could do not to burst into tears. Susan later said that she never recalled that incident without turning "cold and sick at heart."[16]

Susan was the brightest girl at the school, and she loved to learn.[17] Fascinated, she looked through a microscope to study dust on a butterfly's wings. She wrote enthusiastic letters to her family about a Saturday trip to the Philadelphia Academy of Arts and Sciences. Her writing ability, however, suffered at the school. Miss Moulson insisted on reading all the girls' letters before they were sent, and she removed any criticism of the school. Susan tried to send one letter before Miss Moulson approved it, but Miss Moulson found out. She was extremely angry, and Susan felt as if the harsh words from Miss Moulson stopped her from ever writing freely again. Years later, Susan said, "Whenever I take my pen in hand I seem to be mounted on stilts."[18]

At the seminary, Susan made friends with Lydia Mott, whose aunt, Lucretia Mott, occasionally lectured there. Susan had already heard of Lucretia Mott, for Daniel Anthony often spoke approvingly of Mott's antislavery views.

Susan saw a big difference between Deborah Moulson and Lucretia Mott. Strict Deborah Moulson insisted that the girls constantly look within themselves to root out any selfishness or pride. In contrast, Lucretia Mott urged the girls to look beyond themselves and act in ways that benefitted other people in the community. Lucretia Mott followed her own advice. When dissatisfied with the minor role granted women in William Lloyd Garrison's new American Anti-Slavery Society, she organized the Philadelphia Female Anti-Slavery Society. She refused to purchase goods produced by slaveholders, such as cotton cloth or cane sugar.

Throughout Susan's term at the seminary she felt homesick. She never returned to her home, however, because she had none to return to. Like many businesses, Anthony's mill went bankrupt during the 1837 depression. To pay creditors, the house and all its contents were put up for auction.

> Not an article was spared from the inventory. All the mother's wedding presents, the furniture and the silver spoons given her by her parents, the wearing apparel of the family, even the flour, tea, coffee and sugar, the children's school books, the Bible and the dictionary, were carefully noted. . . . [Also included were] "underclothes of wife and daughters;" "spectacles of Mr. and Mrs. Anthony;" "pocketknives of the boys;" "scraps of old iron"—and the law took all except the bare necessities.[19]

Everything was considered the property of the man of the house. Susan saw that even "her mother's things, given her by her own parents, had been seized to pay her father's debts. She would not soon forget the lesson."[20]

At the last minute Lucy Anthony's brother Joshua Read stepped in to help. He bid for all the possessions the family couldn't bear to part with. He told the family to pay him back when they could. When Susan was nineteen, she and her family moved into an abandoned tavern in nearby Hardscrabble, New York.

Susan's happiness seemed to have come to an end. Her family had lost their home. Her beloved Read grandparents, who had lived with her family for the last ten years, died. Adding to Susan's misery was her own low self-esteem caused by the harsh judgments of Deborah Moulson. What could Susan do? Further education was out of the question, because the family could not afford it. In fact, Susan was needed to help support the family.

Living with them at Hardscrabble, she helped build furniture to replace what had been lost in the auction. She "wove carpets, spun great balls of wool and cotton yarn, stitched quilts, and helped her mother and sisters in butter making, cooking, baking . . . and in the entertainment of casual travelers. . . ."[21]

Susan's older sister Guelma became engaged to

Just Do It

"The secret of all my work is that when there is something to do, I do it."[22]

—Susan B. Anthony

Aaron McLean. When they married, she would leave home, reducing her family's expenses. Susan, however, did not look for a husband to support her. She looked for ways to support herself. Although she hated to leave her beloved family, she knew that to help them, she had to go.

3

MORE THAN A SCHOOLMARM

Susan could not sleep. Job Whipple, one of the young men in the neighborhood, had spent the spring evening visiting. Susan had such a good time that she could not shake off her excitement. She woke up after midnight and walked to her window to admire the stars. When she got back in bed, she tossed and turned until about 4:15 A.M., then she gave up on the idea of getting any more sleep.[1] Job Whipple, she wrote, "is a most noble-hearted fellow, kind and courteous in his manners, friendly and obliging to all [and he] has found in me a spirit congenial with his own."[2]

Thoughts of him may have kept Susan awake

most of the night, but in the light of day she knew her first obligation—to help support her family. At nineteen, Susan's childhood was behind her. She accepted a position at a Quaker school for girls in New Rochelle, near New York City.

As she "grew up, she abandoned her middle name in favor of the initial 'B.' and stuck to it consistently."[3] Of course, when she left home in 1839, she had no way of knowing that one day the whole country would recognize her as "Susan B."

She was hired to be a teacher, yet her own education grew from the moment she began her journey down the Hudson River toward New Rochelle, New York. For two hours she listened to antislavery people question slaveholders from Louisiana. Accustomed to hearing antislavery views in her home, she was horrified to hear the Southerners "uphold the institution of slavery."[4]

Before arriving in New Rochelle, she stopped in Brooklyn to attend a Quaker meeting. One of the preachers, Rachel Barker, described the evils of prostitution. Susan B. found the subject shocking, for in those days sex was not considered a proper topic of discussion, much less by a woman in church. But in spite of the subject, Susan B. admired the speaker's skills.[5] She wrote about her to Aaron McLean, with whom she often disagreed about women's equality: "I guess if you could hear her you would believe in a woman's preaching. What an absurd notion that women have not intellectual and moral faculties sufficient for anything but domestic concerns!"[6]

In New Rochelle, Susan B. was angered by some Quakers' racism. At a Quaker meeting she was "shocked by a commotion the Friends [Quakers] made because a black man attended. Some Friends stalked out of the meeting house indignantly. Susan B. exclaimed, 'What a lack of Christianity is this!'"[7] On another occasion, three young black women who were visiting in the area attended the meeting. Susan B. was furious at their reception: "here they are not allowed to sit even on the back seat. One long-faced elder dusted off a seat in the gallery and told them to sit there."[8] Susan made friends with the young women, visiting them and inviting them to tea with her.

Susan B.'s attachment to the Quakers decreased even more after she heard about what happened to her father in Hardscrabble, recently renamed Center Falls. Young people persuaded him to let them hold dances on the third floor of his large home. He reluctantly agreed, because otherwise they would have held them in the town tavern's ballroom. There they would be exposed to alcohol, which Anthony considered a greater evil than dancing. Because of his decision, the antidancing

Friends of Center Falls cancelled Anthony's membership in the church. He said, "For one of the best acts of my life I have been turned out of the best religious society in the world."[9] He still attended meetings, but he grew increasingly committed to individual freedom of thought.

Susan B. had more to do in New Rochelle than reconsider her ties with the Quakers. She taught at Eunice Kenyon's school, which she considered "a good one."[10] In contrast with strict Deborah Moulson, Kenyon was "cheerful and communicative with her scholars [and had] a good heart and a charitable spirit."[11]

When Eunice Kenyon traveled away from the school for a few days, she left Susan B. in charge. A mother of one of the students stopped in for a visit during that time. The mother expressed anger that the young teacher had punished her child by sending her to bed. The criticism brought Susan B. close to tears. The mother threatened to write a letter of complaint to Miss Kenyon. Susan B. hoped the mother would do so, for she believed Miss Kenyon would "not be such a fool as I was to cry, but hold to her rights . . . as she possesses and feels more independence than I fear I ever shall."[12] Susan B.'s fears about her personal strength proved to be unfounded. In the future she would become one of the strongest, most independent women in America.

Teaching the young girls at the school in New Rochelle offered little challenge to Susan B., and in the summer she left the position. She returned to Center Falls in time to attend the wedding of her sister Guelma and Aaron McLean on September 19, 1839. After the wedding, Susan B. accepted a teaching position at a local school, and she enjoyed being close to her family and old friends. However, Aaron McLean continued to irritate her with his conventional views about "proper" roles for women. One day, Susan B. visited the newlyweds, bringing with her some biscuits she had baked. During their conversation she commented with enthusiasm that she had been studying algebra. McLean said, "I'd rather see a woman make biscuits like these than solve the knottiest problem in algebra." Susan B. retorted, "There is no reason why she should not be able to do both!"[13]

Choosing to Remain Single

Susan B. had already shown she was not about to limit herself to concerns of the kitchen. When one

Common Sense Cooking
To make a sponge cake, Susan B. said, "It matters not how good the recipe or the ingredients may be, the cake will not be good unless there is a lot of common sense mixed in with the stir of the spoon!"[14]

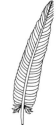

young man proposed that she marry him and give up teaching, she refused. None of her male friendships developed into permanent relationships. When she was in New Rochelle, Susan B. felt puzzled and offended when Job Whipple and two other young men sent her jokes and love poems clipped from a newspaper.[15] She wrote in her diary, "What they mean I can not tell, but silence will prove the best rebuke."[16] Her silence offered no encouragement, and the relationship with Job Whipple went no further.

Because of her slightly crossed eye, Susan B. never considered herself good looking. At age twenty, she underwent an operation to correct the condition. However, Susan B. said the doctor "cut the muscle too much, and that threw the eye the other way."[17] After that, she felt even more self-conscious about the defect, but friends throughout her life described the eye's position as barely noticeable.[18]

One proposal of marriage came from a man she called "a real soft-headed old bachelor" and another from a wealthy widower who said she reminded him of his first wife.[19] Susan B. turned down all her suitors, but she continued her active social life with friends—enjoying picnics, short buggy rides, and extended trips to neighboring villages. Years later, she commented, "I never found the man who was necessary to my happiness. I was very well as I was."[20]

Of course, she spent most of her time in Center Falls earning a living. The former teacher had been fired, yet Susan B. did not receive the same salary he had earned. Instead of ten dollars per week, she made only $2.50. It was normal to pay female teachers only one-fourth of the pay a man earned, even if the woman did the job as well or better.[21]

In the summer of 1845, Susan B.'s younger sister Hannah married Eugene Mosher. After the excitement of the wedding wore off, Susan B. felt lonely. She had always shared a close bond with Guelma and Hannah, the sisters nearest her in age. She missed them terribly now that they were married.[22] One evening Susan B. wrote that she and Hannah "had a good old fashioned chat and cried because we could not all be together."[23]

As a single woman, what kind of life could Susan B. make for herself? She did not yet know.

In November she joined her parents on a westward trip. For a week they camped on top of their belongings, which they had loaded onto an Erie Canal boat. It was pulled by a mule. When they came to low bridges, everybody ducked. The Anthonys' destination was a thirty-two acre farm in Rochester, New York. They purchased it with ten thousand dollars inherited by Susan B.'s mother from her parents, the Reads. Because married women could not own property in their own name, the inheritance passed through Susan B.'s uncle Joshua Read to her father. The family settled into the homestead, planted new fruit trees, and tended the orchards. Daniel Anthony also worked for the New York Life Insurance Company. Once again, the family prospered.

Headmistress

Susan B. did not stay on the farm for long. She took a position as headmistress for girls at the well-known Canajoharie Academy near Albany, New York. Living in Canajoharie with her non-Quaker cousin Margaret and her family, she tried many new luxuries. She no longer wore the plain clothes of the Quakers. She used some of her earnings to buy pretty dresses and shawls.

At the end of the first term, her students took public examinations in front of the principal, the trustees, and the parents. The girls demonstrated what they had—or had not—learned. Susan B.'s skill as a teacher was tested as much as the students' skills. She was so worried the night before that "her nerves were on fire," and she could not sleep a wink.[24]

For the examination, Susan B. made herself a new dress of white, blue, and purple plaid. Her glossy brown hair was arranged in four braids wrapped around a decorative comb. She watched proudly as her students performed well.[25] Many people watched Susan B., too. "All say the schoolmarm looks beautiful."[26] Many observers feared that some young man might take a fancy to the attractive teacher and propose, thus taking her away from the school.

But Susan B. was not ready to abandon her teaching career. She gained more confidence and enjoyed working with the girls.[27] She taught a wide variety of subjects, took her students on field trips, played games, and even wrote and directed a play for them to perform. The townspeople considered her "the smartest woman who ever came to Canajoharie."[28]

Besides trying new fashions and teaching methods, Susan B. also tried dancing. She loved it. However, she disapproved of the drinking that

When she was Headmistress for Girls at the Canajoharie Academy, Susan B. Anthony abandoned plain Quaker clothes, and wore fashionable dresses.

went on at nearly every dance.[29] At one military ball, her fun was spoiled when her date had too much to drink. He stumbled over his feet on the dance floor, and Susan B. wrote, "I certainly shall not attend another dance unless I can have a total abstinence man [nondrinker] to accompany me . . . !"[30]

Susan B. supported temperance, the idea that alcohol should be restricted or outlawed. However, the leading temperance organization in New York State, the Sons of Temperance, did not allow women to join. Determined to participate in spite of the men's attitude, women formed the Daughters of Temperance. Their goal was to end the sale of strong liquor, such as rum and whiskey. Susan B. joined the chapter in Canajoharie, and she formed a new chapter in Albany. At a fund raiser in 1849, she made her first public speech. Intense and earnest, she said the temperance movement would succeed when women united for it. The audience responded with resounding applause.

Susan B. lived happily with Margaret and her family for two years in Canajoharie. But after the birth of her fourth child, Margaret grew ill and died. Susan B. felt tremendous grief after the death of her cousin.[31] She did not want to stay in Canajoharie.[32]

Susan B. craved an outlet for her talents, but what could it be?[33] As a headmistress, she had reached the top of the career ladder in the most respectable field for women. She earned less than a man and had no possibility of further promotion. At this time, the California Gold Rush was at its height, and Susan B. wrote, "Oh, if I were but a man so that I could go!"[34]

Marriage did not offer the freedoms she sought. Married women had virtually no rights, a lesson Susan B. had learned when her mother's personal possessions were auctioned to pay her father's debts in Battenville. Reflecting on her mother's life, Susan B. wrote that she often thought of "the sadness that has long o'shadowed her brow."[35]

At her father's invitation in 1849, Susan B. boarded a train and headed back to Rochester. On the farm, she saw that the young fruit trees the family had planted were now mature. So was Susan B. At twenty-nine, ready to move beyond the role of schoolmarm, she decided to "help right the wrongs of society."[36]

Her life's work was about to begin.

4

FIGHTING FOR THE RIGHT TO FIGHT

In 1850, Rochester was bubbling with debate about one of society's evils, and Susan B.'s family was caught up in the middle of the controversy. The subject of slavery divided the Quakers. The more conservative Friends believed slavery should not be expanded beyond the states where it already existed. Daniel Anthony sided with the radicals who demanded abolition—the immediate end of slavery altogether.

Many of the best abolitionist speakers came to the Anthony farm to discuss their views. Wendell Phillips and William Lloyd Garrison regularly visited, as did the famous former slave, Frederick

Douglass. During Sunday dinners, Susan B. served the guests while she listened to their ideas. Her father said that if he had "the mind and tongue of a Douglass," he would have spoken out against slavery himself.[1] Daniel Anthony was no lecturer, but his daughter Susan B. was. He encouraged her to speak for social reforms.

Susan B. joined the Rochester Daughters of Temperance. Having led the women's temperance movement in Canajoharie and Albany, she put her skills to use in Rochester. She organized fairs, festivals, and suppers. The women were impressed with the way she seemed to "create money out of the air."[2] They elected her as their delegate to many conventions.

In the spring of 1851, on her way home from one

Refining the Swine

At a fund-raiser organized by Susan B., one man proposed this toast to the Daughters of Temperance for their benefits to men:

Our characters they elevate,
Our manners they refine:
Without them we'd degenerate
To the level of the swine.[3]

of these temperance meetings, Susan B. stopped to hear William Lloyd Garrison and George Thompson speak at an antislavery convention in Seneca Falls, New York. She stayed at the home of Amelia Bloomer. Bloomer published *The Lily*, a temperance newspaper "devoted to the interests of women."[4]

Like many temperance supporters, Bloomer saw little connection between liquor reform and the changes proposed by activists supporting a new women's rights movement. Bloomer believed the banning of alcohol would strengthen the family, but she feared that demanding women's rights would weaken it. She considered women's suffrage— women's right to vote—too radical; she called it too "ultra."[5] She tried to avoid women's suffrage workers, but that was not easy. Elizabeth Cady Stanton, the leader of the "ultras," lived in the same town!

Elizabeth Cady Stanton

Elizabeth Cady Stanton had organized the first women's rights convention three years earlier with Lucretia Mott, the abolitionist speaker whom Susan B. had admired when she was a student at Miss Moulson's school. During the two-day meeting in Seneca Falls, Elizabeth Cady Stanton read her Declaration of Rights and Sentiments. She demanded women's equality before the law, in the church, in education, in the family, and in employment. Her most controversial resolution called for women's right to vote.

About three hundred people attended the Seneca Falls convention in 1848. Some were simply curious to hear what they expected would be outlandish demands from wild women who had dared to organize such a novel event. Many people attending were Quakers, generally open-minded in their views compared to the rest of the population. Yet an uproar resulted when Stanton called for women's right to vote. Her husband had refused to come when she told him of her intentions. He said calling for women's suffrage would make the meeting a laughingstock.

At the meeting, Frederick Douglass spoke persuasively in support of the women. As a black man, he understood the pain of being denied the right to vote. After heated debate, all the resolutions passed, even the one calling for women's suffrage. Two weeks later, a convention was held in Rochester. Susan B.'s parents and her younger sister Mary attended that meeting and signed the resolutions.

Susan B. lived in Canajoharie at the time, and her main interest lay with temperance and abolition. But her family wrote her about these first women's rights conventions. Susan B. was curious about women's rights in general and Elizabeth Cady Stanton in particular. She never dreamed that Amelia Bloomer would be the person to introduce them. It happened when they were on their way back to Bloomer's house after attending the abolition lecture in Seneca Falls.

Elizabeth Cady Stanton always remembered the meeting:

> Walking home with the speakers, who were my guests, we met Mrs. Bloomer with Miss Anthony on the corner of the street waiting to greet us. There she stood, with her good earnest face and genial smile, dressed in gray delaine [a type of cloth], hat and all the same color, relieved with pale blue ribbons, the perfection of neatness and sobriety. I liked her thoroughly.[6]

Their friendship quickly grew. Mrs. Stanton (the name Susan B. always used for her) had plunged into the fight for women's rights when she and her husband Henry B. Stanton traveled on their honeymoon to the 1840 World Anti-Slavery Convention in London, England. At the convention, Elizabeth Cady Stanton, Lucretia Mott, and other American women were denied the right to speak. They were allowed only to listen from a distant gallery of the convention hall. The angry women resolved to hold a meeting for discussion and protest when they returned to the United States. Eight years and three children later, Stanton organized the Seneca Falls convention, the first women's rights meeting in America.

Susan B. was drawn to support women's rights in a startlingly similar way. Less than a year after being introduced to Stanton, Susan B. attended a large Sons of Temperance meeting in Albany in 1852. Many women from various branches of the Daughters of Temperance came as well. Accustomed to addressing women's temperance meetings by this time, Susan B. rose to speak. However, the men told her that "the sisters were not invited there to speak but to listen and learn."[7]

Susan B. stalked out of the hall. She organized an alternative meeting for women. She found a church basement to hold it in, and announced the meeting in the evening newspaper. Rallying to her cause, women and supportive men braved the cold January night and gathered in the basement to let their voices be heard. That evening they organized the Woman's State Temperance Society and scheduled a convention in Rochester in the spring. This would be the largest convention Susan B. had ever undertaken. Her new friend, Elizabeth Cady Stanton, promised to deliver the main speech.

The convention was a success. Susan B. presided over all six sessions with "skill and self-assurance."[8] The meeting went smoothly except for the reactions to Stanton's shocking proposal that women be allowed to divorce drunken husbands. Divorce was considered scandalous, and most temperance workers would not support the idea. However, Susan B. somehow persuaded the assembly to elect Stanton president. Susan B. accepted the position of secretary.

Women were invited to future meetings held by the men's temperance organization, but at none of them were women allowed to speak. Clergymen, often the most conservative of temperance supporters, held the most power in the movement. They denounced the idea of women participating actively in any public meeting in which both men and women were present. Each time Susan B. was prevented from speaking, she organized alternative meetings where she addressed large groups of many women and a few men. One woman in Elmira, New York, said she felt shy about addressing a stranger, but she wanted to tell Susan B. that she had done one thing. "And what is that?" asked Susan B. "You have convinced me that it is proper for women to talk Temperance in public as well as in private."[9]

In 1852, Susan B. attended her first National Women's Rights convention. It was held in Syracuse, New York. She admired the impressive speaking skills of Lucy Stone and Antoinette Brown. Like Susan B., these women were not married. Also like her, they had dedicated their lives to social reform. Finally, they had all begun their work in other reforms but had been thrust into women's rights because of the restrictions they faced. They had to fight for the right to fight injustice.

Bloomers

Fashion dictated one such restriction. Women wore long, heavy skirts that made movement slow and cumbersome. To avoid tripping, women used one hand to hold their long skirts up. Stanton's cousin, Elizabeth Smith Miller, designed a new outfit consisting of a short skirt over a pair of very loose-fitting trousers gathered at the ankle. The costume allowed women much more freedom of movement. It freed women's hands and made walking and stair climbing much easier.

Amelia Bloomer liked the safe and sensible clothing. She promoted it in her newspaper. Quickly the new fashion was dubbed "bloomers," but few women dared wear it. Why? Those who did were taunted and laughed at for their "breeches." Bloomer denied that the outfit made her "any the less womanly," but the public outcry continued.[10] "Heads wagged and the tongues wagged as well."[11] Nonetheless, Stanton applauded the outfit. She said,

> To see my cousin, with a lamp in one hand and a baby in the other, walk upstairs with ease and grace, while, with flowing robes, I pulled myself up with difficulty, lamp and baby out of the question, readily convinced me that there was sore need of reform in woman's dress.[12]

This 1851 cartoon makes fun of women wearing bloomers. Women here are also wearing men's hats, smoking cigars, and carrying whips.

When she wore bloomers, Stanton's new and cherished ability to move easily made her feel "like a captive set free from his ball and chain."[13]

Susan B. also began wearing bloomers. However, like the other women, she felt embarrassed by people's reaction to her clothing.

> On the streets of the larger cities the women were followed by mobs of men and boys, who jeered and yelled and did not hesitate to express their disapproval by throwing sticks and stones.[14]

She also tried a new short haircut. Without having to spend hours taking care of her long hair, she had time for issues she deemed more important. In many ways, haircuts and bloomers "represented a sincere revolt on the part of the women."[15] Instead of accepting the conventional fashions, Susan B. and her friends asserted their right to dress as they saw fit. The extent of the ridicule shows how much people were threatened by the women's rebellion, and the rebellion was just beginning.

In June 1853, Susan B. had to make a choice. The moment of decision came at the second convention of the organization Susan B. had begun, the Woman's State Temperance Society. Stanton alarmed the conservative temperance workers when she said, "We have been obliged to preach Woman's Rights because many, instead of listening to what we had to say on Temperance,

Susan B. Anthony cut her hair short, rebelling against traditional expectations of women. About this time, she met Elizabeth Cady Stanton, who helped focus her reform efforts on women's rights.

have questioned the right of women to speak on any subject."[16]

The organization did not exclude men. In fact, at this meeting male members dominated. When the votes were cast for president for the upcoming year, Stanton was not re-elected. Although Susan B. was unanimously re-elected secretary, she refused the position. She resigned from the organization, which soon fell apart without their leadership.

Susan B. recognized that the women's temperance organization simply served to support the men's organization, the one with the real power. She agreed with Stanton that reforming liquor laws was important, but a much larger cause called them: equal rights for women. As Susan B. wrote to Bloomer, "We women are beginning to know that the life and happiness of a woman is of equal value with that of a man."[17]

Susan B. and Elizabeth Cady Stanton shared the commitment to women's rights. However, some of their differences also helped bring them together.

Stanton had a large and growing family. Recognizing the obligations keeping Stanton firmly planted in her home, Susan B. wrote,

> Every wife and mother must devote herself wholly to home duties, washing and cleaning, baking and mending—these are the must be's . . . [and] the thought of anything or anybody beyond the home and family are the may be's.[18]

But she did not consider the situation fair or impossible to change.

> When society is rightly organized, the wife and mother will have time, wish and will to grow intellectually, and will know that the limits of her sphere, the extent of her duties, are prescribed only by the measure of her ability.[19]

In the 1850s, however, neither Susan B. nor Stanton considered society to be "rightly organized," so each did her best given the current "must be's."

Overwhelmed with domestic responsibilities and surrounded by her conservative family, Stanton promoted women's rights in the ways she could. Her father, Daniel Cady, had been a lawyer and judge. Growing up in the Cady household, she had been well trained in the law. Now she applied her understanding of the law to questions affecting women's rights. She read, developed feminist philosophy, and wrote powerful speeches. She formulated the fundamental ideas of the women's movement from her Seneca Falls home.

In contrast, as a single woman, Susan B. was free to travel and lecture to promote women's rights. The liberal Anthony family encouraged her reform work, and her fund-raising skills helped to pay her way.

Susan B. regularly visited the Stanton home in Seneca Falls to discuss with Stanton ways to expand

This portrait, taken in 1856, is of Elizabeth Cady Stanton holding her daughter, Harriot, the sixth of her seven children.

freedoms for women. The Stanton children called her "Aunt Susan." According to Henry Stanton, "Susan stirred the puddings, Elizabeth stirred up Susan, and then Susan 'stirs up the world!'"[20] Elizabeth Cady Stanton put it this way, "I forged the thunderbolts, she fired them."[21]

These two women shaped the women's rights movement for half a century. Together, they changed America.

5

SPEAKING
OUT

When Susan B. set out to do something, she let nothing get in her way—not even bloomers. Traveling, organizing meetings, and speaking to audiences, she found wearing bloomers "a physical comfort but a mental crucifixion . . . an intellectual slavery."[1] Taunted and stared at, she could never stop thinking about her appearance, even when she was giving a speech. She said to her friends,

> The attention of my audience was fixed upon my clothes instead of my words. I learned the lesson then that to be successful a person must attempt but one reform . . . as the average mind can grasp but one idea at a time.[2]

Women's rights was the one idea she wanted people to grasp, so after about a year, she returned to wearing long skirts.

At an 1853 New York State Teachers' meeting, Susan B. stood and addressed Charles Davies, who was presiding over the convention.

> A bombshell would not have created greater commotion. For the first time in all history a woman's voice was heard in a teachers' convention. Every neck was craned and a profound hush fell upon the assembly.[3]

Then the men heatedly debated whether women had the right to speak at the convention—women who paid the same fee as men to be admitted, women who worked in the same profession, women who outnumbered men in it. Although two thirds of the five hundred people attending were women, only the men sat near the front, and only the men spoke. It took them a half hour to decide whether to allow Susan B. to express her opinion. By a slim margin, they voted yes.

In a clear voice, she returned to the original topic the men had been discussing—society's poor attitude toward teachers. She said that teaching was a little-respected profession simply because women were allowed to do it. Women were not thought to have enough intelligence to be doctors or lawyers, so it seemed that anyone who taught—female or male—was not considered very smart!

The meeting soon adjourned. Three men rose from their seats to congratulate Susan B. for her remarks. The newspaper wrote that she had "hit the nail on the head."[4] However, many people, including women, disapproved of her speech. One said, "I was actually ashamed of my sex."[5] Another woman said, "I was so mad at those three men making such a parade to shake hands with her; that will just encourage her to speak again."[6] Indeed it did. The next day Susan B. argued for a resolution in favor of equal pay for women. It passed. However, actually getting equal pay, or even the equal right to speak at conventions, was still a long way off.

As Susan B. traveled to women's rights conventions in Ohio and across New York State, she felt dismayed at what she discovered. Many local chapters of women's temperance organizations had fallen apart, even though she had helped set them up only a few years before. They crumbled because the women had no money. They could not hire lecturers, rent halls, or publish information. Women were essentially silenced if they had no financial support. Working women made such small salaries that they had little to contribute, and married women had no legal right to any of the money they or their husbands earned. Susan B. acted immediately to try to correct the situation.

Property Rights

She called a convention to begin a petition drive to extend property rights to women. She intended to show the legislators that the citizens of New York State wanted women to have control over their own money and property. Setting out the day after Christmas in 1854, Susan B. made a four-month tour to fifty-four of New York State's sixty counties. Braving winter storms, she rode in sleighs, coaches, and trains. Often she trudged through the snow on foot, going from house to house to collect signatures.

Some women slammed the door in her face, saying they "had all the rights they wanted."[7] Susan B. knew they had very few. Employers paid married women's earnings directly to their husbands. A father could apprentice his and his wife's children to whomever he wished, without her consent. He could state in his will what would become of the children upon his death, regardless of the mother's wishes. Susan B.'s petition called for married women to be allowed to keep their own wages and have equal rights with their husbands over their children.

One minister who refused to sign the petition told Susan B. she should not do such work. He looked her over and said that instead of trying to reform the laws, she should marry and have children. Susan B. answered,

> I think it a much wiser thing to secure for the thousands of mothers in this State the legal control of the children they now have, than to bring others into the world who would not belong to me after they were born.[8]

Little did the minister know that she did receive a marriage proposal during the tour. In the snowy Adirondack Mountains in the northern part of the state, a wealthy Quaker whom Susan B. had met in Albany showed her a great deal of attention. He accompanied her on cold coach rides and put a heated plank of wood by her feet to warm them. Sometimes he transported her in his sleigh drawn by a pair of fine gray horses. He took her home for Sunday dinner. Yet at age thirty-five, she responded to his proposal as she had to all others: no.[9]

Susan B. carried her petitions to Albany. She planned to deliver them to the lawmakers and to attend the New York State Women's Rights Convention being held there. The convention attracted so many enthusiastic participants that it stretched from its scheduled two days to two weeks. Elizabeth Cady Stanton gave a speech that Susan B. printed. She distributed copies of it to every member of the state legislature. She also presented the state assembly with the petitions favoring women's property rights. Ten thousand

What's Hers Is His

Susan B. generally traveled alone. However, on one night of her trip around New York State she was accompanied by a coworker. When they stopped at a small inn, a teenaged mother and her infant greeted them. After rocking the baby to sleep, the hostess prepared them a huge supper. Susan B. admired the young mother's embroidery, neat and clean clothing, and well-kept household. At six the next morning the young woman had another huge meal ready. Then, as Susan B. put it,

> for the moral of this story: When we came to pay our bill, the dolt [idiot] of a husband took the money and put it in his pocket. He had not lifted a hand to lighten that woman's burdens, but had sat and talked with the men in the bar room, not even caring for the baby, yet the law gives him the right to every dollar she earns.[10]

people had signed their names to them. She addressed a special committee of the Senate and assembly. She demanded not only property rights but also women's suffrage, the right to divorce, and the right to hold political office. The lawmakers passed none of them.

But Susan B. did not give up. Lucy Stone, also a women's rights supporter, praised Susan B.'s "brave heart that will work on even in the midst of discouragement."[11]

Some people assumed a women's rights speaker

would be an angry, masculine, laughable character. Susan B. proved them wrong. Wearing a simple black dress, with her dark brown hair swept into a bun, she was described as having "pleasing features."[12] Only slightly taller than average at five feet five inches, she had an air of calm self-confidence. She gave "straightforward, no-nonsense, direct speeches."[13] Even newspapers that did not agree with her views praised her clear speaking style. With her bright blue-gray eyes she looked directly at her listeners. One reporter said she "could easily make herself heard by an audience of from two to three thousand persons."[14]

Year after year Susan B. attended the New York State Teachers' Conventions, always arguing for women's right to speak, hold offices, serve on committees, and earn equal pay. She also pushed for educating boys and girls in the higher grades together, and for admitting women to colleges and

Susan B. Shines

A new acquaintance of Daniel Anthony asked if he were the father of Susan B. Anthony, who was growing famous. Anthony remarked to his daughter, "There was a time, Susan, when a daughter might shine by reflected light from her father, but things seem to have changed considerably."[15]

universities along with men. Only a few places, such as Oberlin College in Ohio, had tried coeducation.[16]

Never confident about her writing, Susan B. begged Stanton to write a speech for her to give at the 1856 teachers' convention. Stanton provided the final document, based on the ideas Susan B. listed. The speech argued that boys and girls were intellectually equal and deserved the same opportunities for education. She said, "If they are allowed to attend picnics together, and balls, and dancing schools, and the opera, it certainly will not injure them to use chalk at the same blackboard."[17] Resistant to change, the teachers were shocked. One professor called coeducation "a vast social evil . . . the first step in the school which seeks to abolish marriage."[18]

Campaigning for Abolition

Susan B.'s demands for social change included the ending of slavery. Frederick Douglass had been a family friend for many years, and now Susan B. often shared the speakers' platform with him at abolitionist meetings. For her, the issue was straightforward: "We demand the abolition of slavery because the slave is a human being."[19] The American Anti-Slavery Society hired Susan B. to organize meetings and lectures to try to convince more people to demand an immediate end to

Frederick Douglass, a friend of the Anthony family, was the leader of the abolition movement.

slavery. For the first time since she had been a teacher, she earned a regular salary. However, ten dollars per week plus traveling expenses did not provide enough income for her to update her wardrobe or indulge in any extras. She mended her old clothes and lived as simply as possible. But she maintained her financial independence, a rare situation for a single woman.[20]

Besides speaking against slavery, she also acted directly. She helped runaway slaves on Rochester's underground railroad, a secret group of people who aided slaves fleeing to freedom. She noted in her diary that she "fitted out a fugitive slave for Canada with the help of Harriet Tubman."[21] Tubman, a runaway slave herself, was nicknamed the "Moses of Her People." She led hundreds of slaves to freedom with the support of people like Susan B.

The Anthony family had always opposed slavery. Susan B.'s younger brothers Merritt and Daniel joined John Brown, a radical abolitionist. He used force to avenge the deaths of early antislavery settlers in Kansas. Merritt helped Brown, and for weeks the Anthonys did not know if he had been hurt or killed. Sick with malaria, he had not been well enough to contact anyone. The moment Susan B. heard that Merritt was all right, she wrote him from the farm in Rochester. In her letter she included a description of an unusual fishing trip: "Your fish pole never caught so luscious a basketful as it has this afternoon."[22] Marching through the orchard, she used his fishing pole to hook ripe fruit from the highest boughs that had been out of reach in the regular harvest. After she put the pole away, she filled a basket with her catch—sweet Crawford peaches to share with her family.

Much stronger than the sweet peaches at her farm, however, was the bitter fruit of slavery. In 1859, John Brown led a raid on a federal arsenal in Harpers Ferry, Virginia. He tried to take guns for slaves to use in fighting for their freedom. Brown was arrested and tried for treason. Fearing persecution as supporters of Brown, many of Susan B.'s abolitionist friends went into hiding. Frederick Douglass fled to Canada and then to England for a year. On the day of Brown's hanging, Susan B. courageously led a meeting in Rochester in his honor. She charged fifty cents admission to reduce the likelihood of hecklers attending. About three hundred people came. Susan B. sent the money that was collected to John Brown's widow and children.

The end of the 1850s seemed bleak. Although several wealthy donors gave money to support the women's rights and antislavery movements, Susan B. felt that little progress was being made.[23] Then in 1860, she attended the Albany women's rights convention. She heard that the women's property and guardianship bill would come up before the legislature in the next session. Susan B. and her coworkers had submitted many petitions since the bill failed six years before. She was determined to win the right for married women to keep their wages, their property, and their children. She hurried to Seneca Falls so that she and Stanton could work together on a speech to the legislature. Stanton later said of Susan B.,

> In thought and sympathy we were one, and in the division of labor we exactly complemented each other. In writing we did better work than either could alone. While she is slow and analytical in composition, I am rapid and synthetic. I am the better writer, she the better critic. She supplied the facts and statistics, I the philosophy and rhetoric. . . . Our speeches may be considered the united product of our two brains.[24]

In Albany, Susan B. arranged for Stanton to address the New York State Legislature. Entitled "A Slave's Appeal," the powerful speech explained that married women, like slaves, did not use their own names, could own no property, could not keep their earnings, had no rights to their children, and could not sign contracts. "The prejudice against color . . ." Stanton said, "is no stronger than that against sex."[25] In fact, she pointed out that free men of color could vote and hold property in some states, yet no woman could do either.

The next day, the Married Women's Property

At age thirty-eight, Susan B. Anthony worked for the American Anti-Slavery Society in addition to promoting women's rights.

Act of 1860 passed the New York Assembly. It guaranteed a woman the right to keep her own earnings, to share guardianship of their children with her husband, and to keep her property if she were widowed. Susan B. and Stanton were triumphant. Yet this victory in the war against male domination was about to be overshadowed by the coming Civil War between the North and the South.

6

CIVIL WAR AND *THE* REVOLUTION

Many Northerners blamed antislavery groups for the growing hostility between North and South. Angry mobs often threatened abolitionist speakers. To provide a safe, central location for abolitionists to meet and store documents, Susan B. set up an office called a depository in Albany, New York.

One evening a woman wearing a dark veil entered the office. She identified herself as Mrs. Phelps, wife of a Massachusetts state senator. She was hiding from her husband. He had been having affairs with other women. When she confronted him with the truth, he threw her down the stairs.

His abuse continued. When she threatened to tell authorities, he had her shut up in an insane asylum for a year and a half, even though she was not mentally ill. Then he refused to let her have their son or daughter. Mrs. Phelps asked for help from her brother, a United States senator. But he said, "The child belongs by law to the father and it is your place to submit."[1] Mrs. Phelps went into hiding with her thirteen-year-old daughter, and turned to Susan B. for help. They had never met before, but Phelps had heard much about her.[2]

Susan B. took Phelps and her daughter on a train to New York City where she believed friends would give them a safe place to stay. Arriving too late to present themselves at anyone's door, they went to a hotel. However, they were refused rooms again and again because they were not accompanied by a man. At midnight, when another hotel keeper said that no room was available, Susan B. replied, "I know that is not so!"[3] She refused to leave, even when he threatened to call the police. Finally, he gave them a room. The next day, Susan B. took Phelps and her daughter to many of her friends, yet it was not until ten o'clock that night that she found someone willing to break the law by harboring a "runaway wife."[4]

Word soon got out that Susan B. had helped Phelps and her daughter. Many abolitionists were furious that a person closely tied to their movement had "abducted a man's child," especially when the man was a prominent politician.[5] Susan B. responded, "As I ignore all law to help the slave, so will I ignore it all to protect the enslaved woman."[6] Even William Lloyd Garrison, her dear friend and coworker, did not see the similarity between the legal condition of slaves and all women. He confronted Susan B. at a large meeting. "Don't you know that the law of Massachusetts gives the father the entire guardianship and control of the children?"[7] She answered that the law also gave slaveholders ownership of slaves. She said, "You would die before you would deliver a slave to his master, and I will die before I will give up that child to its father."[8]

Susan B.'s father seemed to be the only man who supported her: "Legally you are wrong, but morally you are right, and I will stand by you."[9] Within a year Senator Phelps found out where his wife and daughter were hiding. He kidnaped the daughter while she was attending church. The mother never gained custody.

Susan B. and Stanton continued to argue for women's right to divorce in cases of a husband's inhuman treatment of his wife, drunkenness, or desertion. But most people, including men in the abolition movement, considered marriage to be well-attended meeting to order. Stanton was elected president of the Women's National Loyal League, and Susan B. was named secretary. The goal was to collect signatures on petitions urging Congress to pass the Thirteenth Amendment to the Constitution. It would prohibit slavery in the United States forever. Susan B. stayed in New York City to manage and organize the operation with Stanton. In slightly over a year, the League collected four hundred thousand signatures, strong evidence that Northern citizens wanted an end to slavery. The petitions helped congressional leaders pass the Thirteenth Amendment.

Peace between the North and the South was restored in 1865, and the Southern states rejoined the Union. Susan B. hoped to win voting rights not only for the freed slaves but for all women, too. She said that "suffrage is the very foundation of liberty [and] without it there can be no real freedom for either man or woman."[15] But one more obstacle to women's "real freedom" was about to be constructed. While Susan B. was visiting her brother Daniel in Kansas, she read a newspaper story about it.

The United States Congress was considering another constitutional amendment. It would give many citizens' rights to freed male slaves. The word "male" had not been used in the Constitution before. Susan B. boarded a train heading east. On her way to New York, she gave speeches supporting universal suffrage—the right of all citizens to vote regardless of their race or sex. However, the pre-war differences between antislavery reformers and women's rights workers surfaced again. Republicans who supported suffrage for male Negroes (as African Americans were then called) told her to stop bringing up women's rights.

Susan B. hurried to New York to meet with Stanton. Then she encouraged all her friends to work for women's rights now that the war had ended. In Boston and New York, she proposed that the American Anti-Slavery Society and women's rights supporters combine into the American Equal Rights Association. Many women liked the idea, but Wendell Phillips, a leading Boston abolitionist, did not. He believed "the Negro's hour" should come first, and the women should wait their turn.[16] Susan B. was furious! Stanton realized that Susan B. had been correct that the women should not have let up in their women's rights work during the war. Stanton asked, "If the leaders in the Republican and abolition camps could deceive us, whom could we trust?"[17]

At a women's rights convention in June, Stanton and Susan B. came with speeches and petitions for women's suffrage. In a question and answer session, Horace Greeley, editor of the influential and liberal *New York Tribune*, showed that he sided with the other antislavery men who abandoned the women's cause after the war. Their first priority was to secure the vote for freed black men. He said, "Miss Anthony, you know the ballot and the bullet go together. If you vote, are you ready to fight?"[18] Susan B. said she would fight just as Greeley had in the Civil War, holding a pen![19] The audience chuckled. When petitions in favor of women's suffrage were presented, Greeley again was embarrassed. The names of the signers were read aloud, and his wife was one of them! The audience laughed, and any chance of Greeley's support for women's rights was gone for good.

In 1867, Kansas, a new state, was considering two constitutional amendments, one giving the vote to Negroes and one giving it to women in the state. This would be the first time women's suffrage had ever been put before the public for a vote. Republicans supported only Negro suffrage, and Democrats opposed both.

Lucy Stone and her husband Henry Blackwell began lecturing for women's suffrage in Kansas. In late summer, Susan B. and Stanton went too. They split up in order to cover as much territory as possible. Roads were few and conditions primitive. Riding in horse-drawn wagons, often sleeping in flea-infested beds, Susan B. adapted to the rugged challenges of prairie travel.

Suffragist Lucy Stone broke tradition when she kept her maiden name after marrying Henry Blackwell.

Touring demanded money. By October, Susan B. had almost none left. Then she received unexpected help from wealthy George Francis Train. He came to Kansas to do something unheard-of for a Democrat: he spoke for women's suffrage. Although Train was a racist who opposed Negro suffrage, he traveled with and supported Susan B. He gave her money to promote the campaign for women's right to vote. A city gentleman, he admired the ease with which she maintained the busy lecture schedule and adjusted to the frontier.

Thousands of workers had swarmed to Kansas to build the railroad. Many of them were Irish or Southern Democrats. Train's down-to-earth, humorous speeches persuaded them to vote for women's suffrage.[20] Thirty thousand Kansas citizens cast their ballots in the November 5, 1867, election. Nine thousand voted for women's suffrage, and ten thousand voted for Negro suffrage. Both measures lost, but Susan B. found the results encouraging. Almost one in three Kansas voters said yes to women's suffrage, only slightly fewer than the number favoring it for former male slaves.

A Women's Rights Newspaper

Train asked Susan B. why she had no newspaper to publish information and ideas supporting her cause. When she said she had no money to start a newspaper, he offered to give it to her. With Stanton's enthusiastic agreement, she accepted Train's offer. The three traveled back East together, stopping along the way to give speeches at the biggest halls they could find, all paid for by Train.

The first issue of the weekly newspaper came out on January 8, 1868. Edited by Stanton and managed by Susan B., it was called *The Revolution*. Its motto declared, "Men, their rights, and nothing more; women, their rights, and nothing less."[21] Stanton said of *The Revolution*, "Radical and defiant in tone, it awoke friends and foes alike to action. Some denounced it, some ridiculed it, but all read it."[22]

Unpredictable and quickly bored, Train left for England. Susan B. wrote in her diary, "My heart sank within me; only our first number issued and our strongest helper and inspirer to leave us!" Yet she quickly rebounded. "This is but another discipline to teach us that we must stand on our own feet."[23] They had little choice.

Other allies had already abandoned the cause. William Lloyd Garrison and Wendell Phillips no longer supported them because of the newspaper's connection with Train, whose racism was well known. Although Train stopped writing for the paper and made his financial contributions privately, many suffrage workers also remained critical of *The*

Revolution because of his early association with it.[24] Even Lucy Stone criticized Susan B. and Stanton for having anything to do with him.

The Fourteenth Amendment to the United States Constitution passed in 1868, giving many rights to freed male slaves. The next year Frederick Douglass urged the passage of a Fifteenth Amendment, guaranteeing them the vote. Susan B. protested, for all women were left out.

When the Internal Revenue Service told Susan B. to pay taxes on *The Revolution*, she reluctantly did so. She reminded the government that as a woman she was unjustly subject to taxation without representation.[25] She was referring to a famous phrase in the Declaration of Independence explaining one reason why American colonists rebelled against England: they were taxed, but they could not vote in English elections. She added that when women succeeded in getting the vote "as they surely will and that very soon" they would treat men better than the men were then treating women.[26] The Fifteenth Amendment passed in 1870. Susan B.'s prediction that women's suffrage would come "very soon" turned out to be wrong. Just how wrong, she did not yet know.

Susan B. dedicated herself to *The Revolution*. She sold ads and newspapers wherever she went. At the White House, she even talked President

Andrew Johnson into subscribing. But after two years, Train no longer bankrolled it because he had been jailed in Europe. Publication of the paper ended because it simply ran out of money. Susan B. vowed to pay its ten-thousand-dollar debt. Her reputation as a speaker was growing, and she planned to make the money by giving paid lectures about women's suffrage. Instead of running her own newspaper, she would soon be written about in newspapers all across the country.

7

ON THE ROAD FOR WOMEN'S RIGHTS

Susan B. used logic and humor to win debates. One time a professor in Bloomington, Indiana, said women should not have the right to vote because they could not fight. Susan B. looked at the young man, who was of small stature. She answered, "The professor talks about the physical disabilities of women; why, I could take him in my arms and lift him on and off this platform as easily as a mother would her baby!"[1] The audience burst into laughter. The professor squirmed in his seat.

For fifty years, Susan B. made many people squirm as she argued for women's rights. Each year began with the convention of the National Woman

Suffrage Association (Susan B. simply called it The National), which she and Stanton founded in 1869. The January meetings were held in Washington, D.C., in order to be near Congress. Susan B. often spoke to a House or Senate committee.

Totally dedicated, she managed almost every aspect of the conventions: choosing speakers, raising money to rent the hall, printing notices, and arranging travel discounts for people attending. Reporters called her style of directing meetings good-natured and fun. If a speaker went on for too long, Susan B. whispered, "Your time's about up, my dear."[2] She never pounded the gavel or rudely interrupted. One newspaper said, "The woman suffragists love her for her good works, the audience for her brightness and wit, and the multitude of press representatives for her frank, plain, open, business-like way."[3]

One time Susan B.'s careful planning did not work out. She allowed Victoria Woodhull to speak at the 1871 convention. Because Woodhull and her sister Tennessee Claflin supported women's suffrage, Susan B. welcomed them to the movement in spite of their wild reputations. Both were divorced, but they continued to share a home with Woodhull's former husband. They were accused of "free love," a moral scandal.[4] In spite of the fact that Woodhull gave a fine speech, the newspapers paid

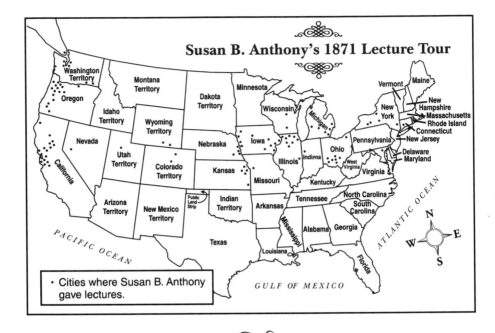

Susan B. Anthony's 1871 Lecture Tour

- Cities where Susan B. Anthony gave lectures.

Susan B. Anthony's 1871-1872 travels began and ended in Washington, D.C., at the annual National Woman Suffrage Association conventions. For half a century, she toured constantly, promoting women's rights in the United States and Europe.

Susan B.'s 1871 Lecture Tour Itinerary[5]

Washington, DC (Jan. 11-13)
Easton, NY (Jan. 16)
Grand Rapids, MI (Jan. 19)
Kansas City, MO (Jan. 23)
Lawrence, KS (Jan. 24)
Topeka, KS (Jan. 25)
Leavenworth, KS (Jan. 26)
Lincoln, NE (Jan. 28-30)
Paola, NE (Jan. 31)
Fort Scott, KS (Feb. 1-2)
Olathe, KS (Feb. 2)
Omaha, NE (Feb. 6)
Council Bluffs, IA (Feb. 7)
Cedar Rapids, IA (Feb. 9)
Toledo, IA (Feb. 10)
Des Moines, IA (Feb. 12-14)
Sterling, IL (Feb. 15)
Dundee, IL (Feb. 16)

Watseka, IL (Feb. 18)
Yellow Springs, OH (Feb. 21)
Springfield, OH (Feb. 22)
Xenia, OH (Feb. 23)
Dayton, OH (Feb. 24)
Salem, OH (Feb. 25)
Columbus, OH (Feb. 27)
Lansing, MI (Mar. 1-2)
Romeo, MI (Mar. 6)
Chicago, IL (Mar. 10-11)
Earlville, IL (Mar. 19)
Mount Pleasant, IA (Mar. 21)
Ottumwa, IA (Mar. 22)
Plattsmouth, NE (Mar. 23)
Nebraska City, NE (Mar. 24)
Burlington, IA (Mar. 27)
Davenport, IA (Mar. 28)
Sycamore, IL (Mar. 29)

Rockford, IL (Mar. 30)
Galena, IL (Mar. 31)
Belvidere, IL (Apr. 1)
Clinton, IA (Apr. 3)
Morrison, IL (Apr. 4)
Princeton, IL (Apr. 5-6)
Lafayette, IN (Apr. 7)
Chicago, IL (Apr. 8-9)
Ripon, WI (Apr. 10)
Jefferson, WI (Apr. 11)
St. Clair, MI (Apr. 14)
Detroit, MI (Apr. 15)
Ann Arbor, MI (Apr. 16)
Hudson, MI (Apr. 17)
Painesville, OH (Apr. 18)
Cuba, NY (Apr. 20)
Rushford, NY (Apr. 22)
Mount Morris, NY (Apr. 24)
New York, NY (May 5-12)
Bridgeport, CT (May 16)
Brookville, PA (June 2)
Xenia, OH (June 5)
Chicago, IL (June 8)
Sioux City, IA (June 14)
Fort Dodge, IA (June 15)
Cherokee, IA (June 16)
Missouri Valley, IA (June 17)
Omaha, NE (June 19-20)
Cheyenne, WY (June 21)
Denver, CO (June 23)
Greeley, CO (June 24)
Cheyenne, WY (June 25)
Laramie, WY (June 26)
Salt Lake City, UT (June 30-July 5)
Corinne, UT (July 7)
San Francisco, CA (July 12)
San Rafael, CA (July 15)
San Jose, CA (July 18)
Yosemite, CA (July 22)
Sondra, CA (July 24)
San Jose, CA (Aug. 3)
Watsonville, CA (Aug. 4)
Santa Cruz, CA (Aug. 5)
Watsonville, CA (Aug. 7)
Woodland, CA (Aug. 17)
Santa Cruz, CA (Aug. 20)
Portland, OR (Sept. 6-11)
East Portland, OR (Sept. 12)
Oregon City, OR (Sept. 13)
Salem, OR (Sept. 14-15)
Milwaukie, OR (Sept. 16)

The Dalles, OR (Sept. 18)
Walla Walla, WA (Sept. 21-23)
Wallula, WA (Sept. 24)
The Dalles, OR (Sept. 25)
Albany, OR (Sept. 27-Oct. 1)
Corvallis, OR (Oct. 2-3)
Monmouth, OR (Oct. 4)
Dayton, OR (Oct. 5)
Lafayette, OR (Oct. 6)
McMinnville, OR (Oct. 7)
Forest Grove, OR (Oct. 9)
Scio, OR (Oct. 10)
Salem, OR (Oct. 12-13)
Olympia, WA (Oct. 17-19)
Tum Water, WA (Oct. 20)
Victoria, BC (Oct. 23-26)
Port Townsend, WA (Oct. 28-30)
Seattle, WA (Nov. 1-3)
Port Madison, WA (Nov. 4-5)
Port Gamble, WA (Nov. 6)
Olympia, WA (Nov. 8-9)
Portland, OR (Nov. 14-15)
Oregon City, OR (Nov. 17)
Eugene, OR (Nov. 19-20)
Oakland, OR (Nov. 22)
Roseburg, OR (Nov. 23-24)
Jacksonville, OR (Nov. 25)
Eureka, CA (Nov. 27-28)
Red Bluff, CA (Nov. 30)
Chico, CA (Dec. 1)
Marysville, CA (Dec. 2)
Sacramento, CA (Dec. 7-8)
Mayfield, CA (Dec. 11)
Oakland, CA (Dec. 12)
San Francisco, CA (Dec. 13)
Healdsburg, CA (Dec. 14)
San Francisco, CA (Dec. 15)
Stockton, CA (Dec. 16)
Nevada City, CA (Dec. 18)
Virginia City, NV (Dec. 20-25)
Laramie City, WY (Jan. 1*)
Cheyenne, WY (Jan. 5*)
Omaha, NE (Jan. 6*)
Chicago, IL (Jan. 8*)
Pittsburgh, PA (Jan. 9*)
Washington, DC (Jan. 10*)

*=1872

more attention to her reputation than to her lecture or those of any of the other suffragists at the National convention that day.[6]

At the same time Woodhull appeared at the National, Lucy Stone set up her own organization, the American Woman Suffrage Association. Stone considered Susan B. and Stanton too radical. Instead of seeking an amendment to the Constitution giving all American women the right to vote, she favored a more conservative strategy. Her organization would try to win women's suffrage state by state. The split in the suffrage movement lasted almost twenty years.

Crossing the Country

Susan B. traveled constantly. She went to California for the first time in 1871. In Chicago, she met Elizabeth Cady Stanton, and together they boarded a train headed west. They stopped and gave speeches all along the way. Once in California, they paused briefly from their lecture schedule to visit Yosemite Valley.

In those days, women usually rode horses sidesaddle, but fifty-one-year-old Susan B. wore bloomers in order to use a man's saddle. She rode a pony down a steep, rugged trail into the Valley. She loved Yosemite's natural beauty. In a letter to her mother she called it a "holy" place.[7]

Most of the holiness in Susan B.'s life involved her reform work. She disagreed with traditional religions that assigned women a silent, supporting role in the church. Abraham Lincoln had said in reference to slavery that "God never made a man good enough to govern other men without their consent."[8] Susan B. said, "God never made a man good enough to govern any woman without her consent."[9] Asked if she ever prayed, she said, "I pray every single second of my life; not on my knees but with my work. My prayer is to lift women to equality with men. Work and worship are one with me."[10]

In 1872, Susan B. tried a new strategy for women's suffrage. Although the Constitution did not say women could vote, it did not say they couldn't. She decided to see what would happen if she voted. She was arrested, tried, and convicted. Even people opposed to women's suffrage were horrified by the unfairness of her trial in which the judge did not let the jury reach a verdict. He told them that he had already

The Fall of Justice
A legend developed in Canandaigua, New York, the town where Susan B. was tried for voting. The Statue of Justice stood high on top of the courthouse dome. People said that the arm of the statue fell to the ground on the day of her sentencing.[11]

THE DAILY GRAPHIC

AN ILLUSTRATED EVENING NEWSPAPER
39 & 41 PARK PLACE

| VOL. VIII. | All the News. Four Editions Daily | NEW YORK, THURSDAY, OCTOBER 21, 1875.—TWELVE PAGES. | $12 Per Year in Advance. Single Copies, Five Cents. | NO. 816. |

REAL vs. IMAGINARY WANTS.

Misses Anthony and Dickinson and Mrs. Stanton—"We hold that this gives women the right to vote. Any way, you might let us."
Chief Justice Waite—"In the opinion of the Court the XIV. Amendment does not confer on women the right of suffrage."
Public Opinion—"And you might add, Mr. Chief Justice, that the great question of the day is, How to improve the suffrage—not how to extend it."

Many newspapers mocked suffragists. This 1875 cartoon shows Susan B. Anthony, Elizabeth Cady Stanton, and Anna Dickinson wearing men's shorts and trousers.

decided she was guilty. Susan B. never paid the fine for the crime of voting.

At the conclusion of the trial, she hit the campaign trail again. She traveled by railroad, sleigh, ship, wagon, and coach; in heat, rain, and snow. Some of the dirt roads she called rough as "corduroy."[12] A different kind of rough road, however, was her struggle to earn enough to repay the 1870 debt for *The Revolution*. On May 1, 1876, she finally paid off the last of the ten thousand dollars. Newspaper editors who did not agree with her women's rights views still applauded her. One said they should "raise their hats in reverence" to her.[13] When it was suggested that she had paid her debt "like a man," the *Buffalo Express* said "Not so," for a man "would have settled at ten or twenty cents on the dollar." She paid the full amount.[14] The *New York Graphic* noted how hard she had worked to earn the money. In one year alone she lectured one hundred twenty times. The paper said her diligence and "personal honor" made her "thoroughly qualified to plead for the claims of her own sex."[15]

Yet many people still did not want to hear those claims.

A Century of Freedom for Men

The planners of the nation's centennial, its one hundredth birthday celebration, refused to give

Susan B. or any suffragist a chance to speak during the proceedings in Philadelphia on July 4, 1876.

Money was not the problem. As chairman of the campaign committee, Susan B. combined a fund-raising drive for the centennial with a project that she, Elizabeth Cady Stanton, and Matilda Joslyn Gage had in mind. They planned to write a history of the women's suffrage movement, expecting it to be a book of several hundred pages. To anyone who sent them five dollars, the authors promised a book upon its completion. In the meantime, the money would be used to set up a temporary headquarters for the National in Philadelphia. Enough money was soon received. Susan B. rented the rooms because she was the only woman in the group who could legally do so: Pennsylvania law did not allow a married woman to sign a contract. But the women were denied permission to speak at the celebration. Susan B. asked if they could silently present a written declaration of women's rights. Again, the answer was no. But that did not stop Susan B.

She had four regular admission tickets and a pass to attend the event as a reporter for her brother's newspaper. She and four officers of the National entered the huge assembly hall and took their seats. After the 1776 Declaration of Independence was read, Susan B. led the four officers to the speakers' platform. They carried copies of their Declaration

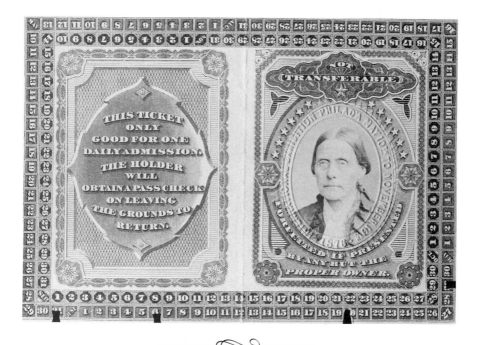

Susan B. Anthony used this ticket to enter the Centennial Celebration in 1876.

of Rights for Women. Susan B. presented one to the Chairman of the Centennial Celebration. Surprised and angry, he bellowed "Order, order!"[16] On their way out, Susan B. and the other women distributed copies of the document to the eager, outstretched hands of the audience.

Then they went to Independence Hall where Stanton and many supporters were waiting for them. In her loud, strong voice, Susan B. read the Declaration of Rights for Women in front of the Liberty Bell inscribed with the words, "Proclaim liberty

Although her expression makes her look somber, Susan B. was known for her wit and good humor. People had to sit motionless for many minutes to pose for a photograph, and holding a smile that long was almost impossible.

throughout all the land unto all the inhabitants thereof."[17] While the men at the official celebration spoke of their hundred years of rights and freedoms, Susan B. listed the many rights still denied one half the citizens, such as the right to vote, make contracts, receive equal treatment within the legal system, and not be taxed without representation. Amid much applause, Susan B. concluded, "We ask justice, we ask equality, we ask that all the civil and political rights that belong to citizens of the United States, be guaranteed to us and our daughters forever."[18]

For Susan B., having an idea usually led to immediate action. Even before a single line of *The History of Woman Suffrage* had been written, she looked for a publisher. Then she, Stanton, and Gage worked together for months on *The History*. The first volume, 871 pages long, was released in 1881 and received good reviews.[19] Soon they began volume two. The project grew, as did the suffrage movement. The Women's Christian Temperance Union under the leadership of Emma Willard at first had shied away from the suffrage issue, but in 1881 finally endorsed it. The liquor industry, fearing that female voters would outlaw alcohol, formed much of the strongest opposition to women's suffrage.

At age sixty-three, Susan B. made her first trip to Europe, accompanying Elizabeth Cady Stanton. At a crowded farewell reception in her honor, Susan B. said,

> I have known nothing the last thirty years save the struggle for human rights on this continent. . . . I hope while abroad that I shall do something to recommend our work here, so as to make them respect American women and their demand for political equality.[20]

During her ten months in Europe she was honored for her achievements in the United States. But her main goal had yet to be reached. Upon her return, she continued working and touring for suffrage, which she always referred to as "the cause." She reminded Congress in 1884 that this was the fifteenth year that women had come before them requesting suffrage.

The year 1887 marked the first time the women's suffrage amendment, the Sixteenth Amendment, ever made its way out of committee and to Congress for a vote. It was defeated, but Susan B. was not.

8

FAILURE IS
IMPOSSIBLE

S usan B. still worked hard for the cause well into
her seventies. She continued to travel and
lecture. Younger women flocked to her, eager to
learn all they could about leading the movement.
Rachel Foster, May Wright Sewall, Anna Howard
Shaw, and Carrie Chapman Catt revered her.
Sometimes she was affectionately known as General
Anthony.

To celebrate the fortieth anniversary of the
Seneca Falls Convention in which Stanton first
demanded women's right to vote, Susan B. issued a
call to establish the International Council of Women
in 1888. What a response she received! Fifty-three

In the Arms of Susan B.
In Lincoln, Kansas, a mother explained to Susan B. that she had brought her four-week-old daughter "twenty-five miles in a carriage, so she might tell it, when grown, that Susan B. Anthony had taken it in her arms."[1]

organizations sent representatives. They came from Europe, Canada, and the United States. To Susan B.'s great pleasure, Lucy Stone and her rival American Woman Suffrage Association came too. Susan B. said, "We are to stand together again after these twenty years. But none of the past! Let us rejoice in the good of the present, and hope for more and more in the future."[2]

Susan B. welcomed the assembled people and then introduced Mrs. Stanton. The audience stood as they applauded. After Stanton's speech, Susan B. called to the stage Frederick Douglass, one of the original signers of the 1848 Declaration of Sentiments. The formation of the International Council marked the unity of the old antislavery reformers, Lucy Stone's American Woman Suffrage Association, and the National. The next year, the National-American Woman Suffrage Association (NAWSA) officially merged the two suffrage groups. The work went on.

Women's Suffrage in the State of Wyoming

One evening in 1890, as she was lecturing during a tour of South Dakota, Susan B. was handed a telegram. What could be so important that it could not wait until she left the lecture stage? She read the telegram to the audience. It said that the Wyoming Territory, which had granted women suffrage in 1869, had just been admitted as a state— the first in the nation to allow women to vote! Mary Seymour Howell, who also stood on the platform, later said Susan B. was so overjoyed by the news that

> the very tones of her voice changed; there were ringing notes of gladness and tender ones of thankfulness. It was the first great victory of her forty years of work. She spoke as one inspired, while the audience listened for every word, some cheering, others weeping.[3]

Susan B. traveled across the country again in 1895. After her campaign in California, suffrage lost in that state by only a slight margin. Although seventy-five years old, she maintained a heavy schedule. Then as she finished a speech on July 26 in Lakeside, Ohio, she collapsed. She had fainted from exhaustion. Journalists swarmed to the Anthony home in Rochester to see if Susan B.'s sister, Mary, knew what had happened. One Chicago paper telegraphed its reporter about how long an article to write: "50,000 words if still living, no limit, if dead."[4] She lived.

No. 1,732.—Vol. LXVII.] NEW YORK—FOR THE WEEK ENDING NOVEMBER 24, 1888. [PRICE, 10 CENTS.

WOMAN SUFFRAGE IN WYOMING TERRITORY.—SCENE AT THE POLLS IN CHEYENNE.
FROM A PHOTO. BY KIRKLAND.—SEE PAGE 253.

Women voting in Wyoming Territory made front page news. When Wyoming became a state in 1890, it was the first that allowed women's suffrage.

Susan B. slowed down some, but she continued planning a grand eightieth birthday celebration for Elizabeth Cady Stanton. A few weeks after the celebration with its overflow crowd of well-wishers, Stanton released her *Woman's Bible.* The radical book interpreted the Bible to show women as men's equals. It offended many younger suffragists who wanted to distance themselves from its author. Susan B. told them that religious freedom was a right to uphold. She reminded them that in the early days of the movement, many of Stanton's ideas had been considered shocking, but by the end of the century they were accepted. Similarly, Stanton's views on the Bible might not seem radical in years to come.

One of the first reforms Susan B. Anthony and Elizabeth Cady Stanton had fought for was simply the right to speak out. Since then, they

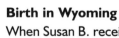

Birth in Wyoming
When Susan B. received a birth announcement from the governor of Wyoming, she asked if the baby was a boy or girl. He answered, "No matter which. We are in Wyoming."[5]

Susan B. Anthony (center) had ridden into Yosemite Valley before at age fifty-one. As shown here, she did it again in 1895 at age seventy-five.

had addressed hundreds of audiences. Susan B. said,

> It would be hard to find a city in the northern and western States in which I have not lectured, and I have spoken in many of the southern cities. I have been on the platform over forty-five years and it would be impossible to tell how many lectures I have delivered; they probably would average from seventy-five to one hundred every year. I have addressed the committees of every Congress since 1869, and our New York legislature scores of times.[6]

A Half Century for Women's Rights

At the 1898 NAWSA conference, Susan B. stood by an old-fashioned round mahogany table. The table had been shipped there just for the occasion. Seated at that very table, Elizabeth Cady Stanton had written the Declaration of Rights and Sentiments for the first women's rights convention fifty years before. In a half century of work, what progress had women made besides earning the freedom to speak in public?

Most states had expanded property rights for married women, although their filing for divorce and maintaining custody of children were still very difficult.[7] Colorado, Idaho, and Utah had joined

Spring for Susan B.

Susan B. wore a red shawl so often that it became her trademark. When she wore a white one at a session of the 1898 NAWSA convention, a reporter joked about the absence of the familiar symbol, "No red shawl, no report."[8] Susan B. laughed, read the note aloud, and sent for the red shawl. When she wrapped it around her shoulders, the audience burst into applause. One reporter wrote, "Spring is not heralded in Washington by the approach of the robin red-breast but by the appearance of Miss Anthony's red shawl."[9]

Wyoming as states in which women could vote, yet the majority of American women could not. Many professions were opening to women, but in general, women's jobs were still inferior to men's and paid far less.

By 1900, many colleges accepted women. Thanks to Susan B. Anthony, the University of Rochester admitted female students in 1900. The trustees voted to accept them if one hundred thousand dollars was provided to pay for expanded facilities. A local committee did its best to raise the money, but on the eve of the deadline, they were still eight thousand dollars short of the amount needed.

Susan B. acted immediately. The next day she startled the trustees when she appeared at their meeting. She had raised the balance of the money! When the trustees questioned the value of one of the pledges for two thousand dollars, Susan B. offered her life insurance as a guarantee. Susan B. wrote in her diary, "Well they let the girls in—said there was no alternative."[10]

In 1900, on the eve of her eightieth birthday, she retired from the presidency of the National-American Woman Suffrage Association the (NAWSA), which she had held since Stanton's retirement in 1892. Susan B. recommended Carrie

Chapman Catt as her successor. In 1902 Susan B. wrote in her last letter to Stanton:

> We little dreamed when we began this contest, optimistic with the hope and buoyancy of youth, that half a century later we would be compelled to leave the finish of the battle to another generation of women. . . . These strong young women will take our place and complete our work. There is an army of them, where we were but a handful. . . . And we, dear old friend, shall move on the next sphere of existence—higher and larger, we cannot fail to believe, and one where women will not be placed in an inferior position, but will be welcomed on a plane of perfect intellectual and spiritual equality.[11]

Elizabeth Cady Stanton died a few days later at age eighty-six. Susan B. had said a dozen years before,

> I never expect to know any joy in this world equal to that of going up and down the land, getting good editorials written, engaging halls, and circulating Mrs. Stanton's speeches. If I have ever had any inspiration she has given it to me. . . .[12]

At the end of 1902, Susan B. completed the fourth volume of *The History of Woman Suffrage*, which she had written with Stanton, Gage, and Ida Husted Harper, Susan B.'s biographer. But more history was still to be made.

Well into her eighties, Susan B. continued to promote the cause. When she entered the NAWSA convention in 1903, the audience burst into applause and rose to their feet. Susan B. wondered what prompted the excitement. "What has

Susan B. Anthony (standing) and Elizabeth Cady Stanton devoted their long lives to promoting women's rights in general and women's suffrage in particular. This photo was taken about 1880.

happened?" she asked Anna Shaw. "You happened," was the reply.[13]

She continued to happen. Again she traveled across the country, and again to Europe, speaking to large, appreciative audiences. Some admirers referred to her as "Saint Susan"[14] and others dubbed her a "queen."[15] In 1904, President Theodore Roosevelt honored her eighty-fourth birthday at a White House reception. In her typically modest way, Susan B. focused on her work rather than on herself. She said, "I would rather have him say a word to Congress for the cause than to praise me endlessly."[16]

She asked the president,

Mr. Roosevelt, this is my principal request—it is almost the last request I shall ever make of anybody. Before you leave the presidential chair, recommend Congress to submit to the Legislatures a Constitutional Amendment which will enfranchise women, and thus take your place in history with Lincoln, the great emancipator.[17]

Roosevelt did not grant the request.

At her eighty-sixth birthday celebration at the 1906 NAWSA convention, Susan B. spoke her last public words. With her hand on the shoulder of Anna Shaw, the president of NAWSA, Susan B. urged the next generation to continue the work. She declared, "Failure is impossible!"[18]

9

THE WORK GOES ON

During Susan B.'s last days, Anna Shaw sat by her bedside. Susan B. told her, "Remember that the only fear you need have is the fear of not standing by the thing you believe to be right. Take your stand and hold it: then let come what will, and receive the blows like a good soldier."[1] She made only one complaint from her death bed: "I have been striving for over sixty years for a little bit of justice no bigger than that, and yet I must die without obtaining it. Oh, it seems so cruel!"[2] Shaw comforted her, "Your grand struggle has changed life for women everywhere."[3]

What changes had been made? A few weeks

earlier, Professor Lucy Salmon of Vassar College listed some of the accomplishments of Susan B. and her coworkers:

> We are indebted to them in large measure for the educational opportunities of today. We are indebted to them for the theory, and in some places for the reality, of equal pay for men and women when the labor performed is the same. We are indebted to them for making it possible for us to spend our lives in fruitful work rather than in idle tears. We are indebted to these pioneer women for the substitution of a positive creed for inertia and indifference [women taking an active rather than a passive role in society]. And from them we also inherit the weighty responsibility of passing on to others in degree, if not in kind [the energy, but not necessarily the same specific issues], all that we have received from them.[4]

Shaw asked Susan B. whether she would do the same if she had her life to live again? With no hesitation, she answered, "Oh, yes, I'd do it all again!"[5]

Susan B. died of pneumonia at her home in Rochester, New York, on March 13, 1906. She was eighty-six.

The Central Presbyterian Church was chosen as the funeral site because of its large size, but it still could not seat all the mourners. Ten thousand people braved a heavy snow storm in order to honor the woman who "had aimed at being the emancipator of her sex."[6] Mrs. R. Jerome Jeffrey spoke on behalf of the many African Americans attending: "She was our friend for many years—our champion."[7]

At the conclusion of the speeches, the church doors were opened. Hundreds more people entered and filed past the casket. One elderly woman was "hobbling on a crutch and assisted by one of the ushers; she had been standing outside in the storm so long that she was completely covered with snow,

Stones placed on Susan B. Anthony's simple gravestone in Rochester are a sign of respect. She said in reference to her funeral, "Remember that I want there should be no tears. Pass on, and go on with the work."[8]

The Greatest Revolution

Carrie Chapman Catt said of Susan B. Anthony, "Her eighty-six years measure a movement whose results have been more far-reaching in the change of conditions, social, civil and political, than those of any war of revolution since history began."[9]

and as she gazed on Miss Anthony's face she sobbed aloud."[10] One observer wrote of the mourners who had waited quietly outside, "They were the plain people, the people whom Abraham Lincoln and Susan Anthony loved, and who returned that love without making many words about it."[11]

Anna Howard Shaw gave the last farewell at the grave site. She said that Susan B.'s "cause, perfect equality of rights, of opportunity, of privilege for all, civil and political—was to her the bed-rock upon which all true progress must rest."[12] One suffragist later commented that Susan B., unmarried and childless, was the "mother of us all,"[13] for she had nurtured the women's movement from its infancy.

The Cause Lived On

Susan B. had proclaimed that failure was impossible, and that "by and by there will be victory."[14] To help bring it about, she willed all of her money, forty-five

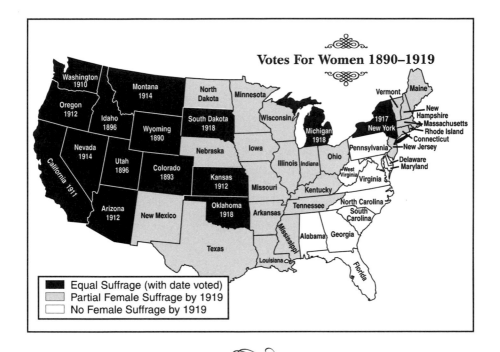

Votes For Women 1890–1919

Washington 1910
Oregon 1912
Idaho 1896
Nevada 1914
California 1911
Utah 1896
Arizona 1912
Montana 1914
Wyoming 1890
Colorado 1893
New Mexico
North Dakota
South Dakota 1918
Nebraska
Kansas 1912
Oklahoma 1918
Texas
Minnesota
Iowa
Missouri
Arkansas
Louisiana
Wisconsin
Illinois
Indiana
Kentucky
Tennessee
Mississippi
Alabama
Georgia
Michigan 1918
Ohio
West Virginia
Virginia
North Carolina
South Carolina
Florida
Pennsylvania
New York 1917
Vermont
Maine
New Hampshire
Massachusetts
Rhode Island
Connecticut
New Jersey
Delaware
Maryland

■ Equal Suffrage (with date voted)
▨ Partial Female Suffrage by 1919
□ No Female Suffrage by 1919

Beginning in 1890 with Wyoming, states began to grant women the right to vote.

hundred dollars, to the cause. But when would victory come?

"The path blazed by Miss Anthony nearly sixty years ago is now an easy one to follow," the New York *World* wrote in 1906. "There are few dangers to be encountered now in the wilderness of woman's rights; in fact it is not a wilderness any more but a land of promise well settled by many citizens."[15]

Two more states granted women suffrage a few years after Susan B.'s death. Washington in 1910 and California in 1911 brought the total number of states in which women could vote to six.

When the United States sent soldiers to Europe to fight in World War I, increasing numbers of American women entered the work force at home. They produced the goods that helped win the war in 1918.

In 1919, the United States Congress finally passed an amendment granting all American women the right to vote. But it would not be added to the Constitution until at least thirty-six states also passed it. Suffragists campaigned hard for another year. Tennessee became the needed thirty-sixth state to approve the amendment in a very close vote: forty-nine to forty-seven.

Originally proposed in 1878 as the Sixteenth Amendment, women's right to vote was added to the Constitution as the Nineteenth Amendment in 1920—one hundred years after Susan B.'s birth. It said, "The right of citizens of the United States to vote shall not be denied or abridged by the United States or by any state on account of sex."[16] It was nicknamed the "Susan B. Anthony Amendment."

The National-American Woman Suffrage Association was transformed into the League of Women Voters in 1920.[17] Still functioning today, its goal is to improve the political process by encouraging the active and informed participation of citizens in government.

Women are urging legislators to move this statue of Elizabeth Cady Stanton, Susan B. Anthony, and Lucretia Mott from the crypt under the United States Capitol to the rotunda alongside the statue of George Washington.

The Susan B. Anthony dollar was first minted in 1979.

Winning the right to vote did not bring women equality in all parts of society. The National Organization for Women (NOW) was formed in 1966 in order to work for "true equality for all women in America and toward a fully equal partnership of the sexes."[18] This resurgence of national interest in women's rights prompted Dr. Alan Goldman of the United States Mint to portray a woman on an American coin.[19] In 1979 and 1980, the Mint issued the Susan B. Anthony dollar to honor her legacy.

Many feminists today belong to national, state, and local organizations that promote equal rights for women in education, employment, religion, health care, and government. Standing on the shoulders of Susan B. Anthony, they "go on with the work."[20]

CHRONOLOGY

1820—Born in Adams, Massachusetts, on February 15.

1826—Moves with her family to Battenville, New York.

1838—Attends Miss Deborah Moulson's Female Seminary for one term.

1839—Teaches for about ten years at various schools throughout New York State.

1849—Begins giving public lectures on temperance; Gives up teaching to live with her family in Rochester, New York.

1851—Meets Elizabeth Cady Stanton in Seneca Falls, New York.

1853—Resigns from the Women's State Temperance Society, which she had founded, in order to focus on women's rights.

1853—Manages and speaks in women's rights and
–1861   antislavery campaigns across New York State.

1863—With Elizabeth Cady Stanton, establishes the
–1867   Women's Loyal League to petition Congress for a permanent end to slavery.

1867—Travels widely, campaigning for women's suffrage
–1905   across the United States.

1868—Publishes *The Revolution*, a newspaper which
–1870   supported women's rights.

1869—With Elizabeth Cady Stanton, founds the National Woman Suffrage Association.

1872—Is arrested for voting in Rochester, New York.

1876—Reads the Declaration of Rights for Women in front of the Liberty Bell, outside the official Centennial Celebration in Philadelphia.

1881—Completes the first of three volumes of *The History of Woman Suffrage* written with Elizabeth Cady Stanton and Matilda Joslyn Gage.

1888—Founds the International Council of Women.

1892—Is president of the National-American Woman
–1900   Suffrage Association.

1902—Completes the fourth volume of *The History of Woman Suffrage*, written with Elizabeth Cady Stanton, Matilda Joslyn Gage, and Ida Husted Harper.

1906—Dies at age eighty-six at her home in Rochester, New York, on March 13.

1920—Nineteenth Amendment, granting women's right to vote, is added to the Constitution.

CHAPTER NOTES

Chapter 1

1. Elisabeth Griffith, *In Her Own Right: The Life of Elizabeth Cady Stanton* (New York: Oxford University Press, 1984), p. 154.

2. Ibid.

3. Lynn Sherr, *Failure Is Impossible: Susan B. Anthony in Her Own Words* (New York: Random House, 1995), p. xvii.

4. Ibid., p. 61.

5. Ida Husted Harper, *Life and Work of Susan B. Anthony* (New York: Arno and *The New York Times*, 1969), p. 437.

6. Griffith, p. 154.

7. Kathleen Barry, *Susan B. Anthony: A Biography of a Singular Feminist* (New York: New York University Press, 1988), p. 255.

8. Ilene Cooper, *Susan B. Anthony* (New York: Franklin Watts, 1984), p. 94.

9. Ibid.

10. Harper, p. 443.

11. Jules Archer, *Breaking Barriers: The Feminist Revolution from Susan B. Anthony to Margaret Sanger to Betty Friedan* (New York: Viking, 1991), p. 57.

12. Harper, p. 444.

13. Archer, p. 57.

14. Sherr, p. 107.

15. Ibid.

16. Barry, p. 250.

17. Ibid.

18. Cooper, p. 90.

19. Sherr, p. 108.

20. Harper, p. 426.

21. Barry, p. 252.

22. Harper, p. 436.

23. Barry, p. 254.

24. Sherr, p. xxii.

25. Archer, p. 56.

26. Eleanor Flexner, *Century of Struggle: The Woman's Rights Movement in the United States* (New York: Atheneum, 1973), p. 166.

27. Ibid., p. 109.

28. Harper, p. 436.

Chapter 2

1. Kathleen Barry, *Susan B. Anthony: A Biography of a Singular Feminist* (New York: New York University Press, 1988), p. 8.

2. Ibid.

3. Ibid.

4. Ida Husted Harper, *Life and Work of Susan B. Anthony* (New York: Arno and *The New York Times*, 1969), p. 14.

5. Katharine Anthony, *Susan B. Anthony: Her Personal History and Her Era* (Garden City, N.Y.: Doubleday, 1954), p. 26.

6. Ibid.

7. Barry, p. 16.

8. Harper, p. 18.

9. Anthony, p. 35.

10. Barry, p. 19.

11. Ibid., p. 20.

12. Jules Archer, *Breaking Barriers: The Feminist Revolution from Susan B. Anthony to Margaret Sanger to Betty Friedan* (New York: Viking, 1991), p. 27.

13. Ibid.

14. Anthony, p. 42.

15. Harper, p. 29.

16. Ibid., p. 31.

17. Rheta Childe Dorr, *Susan B. Anthony: The Woman Who Changed the Mind of a Nation* (New York: AMS Press, 1928), p. 23.

18. Ibid., p. 25.

19. Harper, p. 35.

20. Anthony, p. 57.

21. Dorr, p. 25.

22. Lynn Sherr, *Failure Is Impossible: Susan B. Anthony in Her Own Words* (New York: Random House, 1995), p. 208.

Chapter 3

1. Katharine Anthony, *Susan B. Anthony: Her Personal History and Her Era* (Garden City, N.Y.: Doubleday, 1954), p. 59.

2. Ibid.

3. Ibid., p. 19.

4. Ida Husted Harper, *Life and Work of Susan B. Anthony* (New York: Arno and *The New York Times*, 1969), p. 38.

5. Anthony, p. 60.

6. Harper, p. 40.

7. Ibid., p. 39.

8. Ibid.

9. Ibid., p. 37.

10. Anthony, p. 64.

11. Ibid.

12. Ibid., p. 65.

13. Harper, p. 44.

14. Lynn Sherr, *Failure Is Impossible: Susan B. Anthony in Her Own Words* (New York: Random House, 1995), p. 281.

15. Anthony, p. 60.

16. Ibid., p. 61.

17. Ibid., p. 67.

18. Ibid., p. 68.

19. Kathleen Barry, *Susan B. Anthony: A Biography of a Singular Feminist* (New York: New York University Press, 1988), p. 37.

20. Sherr, p. 13.

21. Harper, p. 45.

22. Barry, p. 43.

23. Ibid.

24. Harper, p. 50.

25. Barry, p. 45.

26. Ibid.

27. Ibid.

28. Harper, p. 55.

29. Ibid., p. 51

30. Ibid.

31. Ibid., p. 52.

32. Ibid.

33. Barry, p. 50.

34. Harper, p. 52

35. Barry, p. 48.

36. Harper, p. 60.

Chapter 4

1. Katharine Anthony, *Susan B. Anthony: Her Personal History and Her Era* (Garden City, N.Y.: Doubleday, 1954), p. 92.

2. Ida Husted Harper, *Life and Work of Susan B. Anthony* (New York: Arno and *The New York Times*, 1969), p. 63.

3. Anthony, p. 99.

4. Harper, p. 63.

5. Anthony, p. 100.

6. Harper, p. 64.

7. Ibid., p. 65.

8. Anthony, p. 103.

9. Ellen Carol DuBois, *The Elizabeth Cady Stanton–Susan B. Anthony Reader* (Boston: Northeastern University Press, 1992), p. 39.

10. Lynn Sherr, *Failure Is Impossible: Susan B. Anthony in Her Own Words* (New York: Random House, 1995), p. 189.

11. Ibid.

12. Elizabeth Cady Stanton, *Eighty Years and More* (New York: Schocken Books, 1971), p. 201.

13. Ibid.

14. Harper, p. 115.

15. Anthony, p. 110

16. Ibid., p. 105.

17. DuBois, p. 40.

18. Sherr, p. 8.

19. Ibid.

20. Elisabeth Griffith, *In Her Own Right: The Life of Elizabeth Cady Stanton* (New York: Oxford University Press, 1984), p. 74.

21. Ibid.

Chapter 5

1. Ida Husted Harper, *Life and Work of Susan B. Anthony* (New York: Arno and *The New York Times*, 1969), p. 117.

2. Ibid.

3. Ibid., p. 98.

4. Lynn Sherr, *Failure Is Impossible: Susan B. Anthony in Her Own Words* (New York: Random House, 1995), p. 20.

5. Ibid.

6. Ibid.

7. Harper, p. 108.

8. Ibid.

9. Kathleen Barry, *Susan B. Anthony: A Biography of a Singular Feminist* (New York: New York University Press, 1988), p. 100.

10. Sherr, p. 47.

11. Harper, p. 111.

12. Barry, p. 101.

13. Ibid., p. 103.

14. Ibid., p. 102.

15. Sherr, p. xxii.

16. Barry, p. 127.

17. Sherr, p. 23.

18. Ibid.

19. Ibid., p. 33.

20. Katharine Anthony, *Susan B. Anthony: Her Personal History and Her Era* (Garden City, N.Y.: Doubleday, 1954), p. 133.

21. Sherr, p. 33.

22. "Fresh Fruit," *Papers of Elizabeth Cady Stanton & Susan B. Anthony, Project News*, Winter 1995, p. 2.

23. Barry, p. 134.

24. Elizabeth Cady Stanton, *Eighty Years and More* (New York: Schocken Books, 1971), p. 166.

25. Elizabeth Cady Stanton, "Address to the New York State Legislature, 1860," In *Feminism: The Essential Historical Writings*, ed. Miriam Schneir (New York: Random House, 1972), p. 119.

Chapter 6

1. Ida Husted Harper, *Life and Work of Susan B. Anthony* (New York: Arno and *The New York Times*, 1969), p. 201.

2. Rheta Childe Dorr, *Susan B. Anthony: The Woman Who Changed the Mind of a Nation* (New York: AMS Press, 1928), p. 138.

3. Kathleen Barry, *Susan B. Anthony: A Biography of a Singular Feminist* (New York: New York University Press, 1988), p. 143.

4. Ibid.

5. Ibid.

6. Harper, p. 204.

7. Ibid.

8. Ibid.

9. Ibid.

10. Lynn Sherr, *Failure Is Impossible: Susan B. Anthony in Her Own Words* (New York: Random House, 1995), p. 16.

11. Ibid.

12. Ibid., p. 47.

13. Elizabeth Cady Stanton, *Eighty Years and More* (New York: Schocken Books, 1971), p. 254

14. Sherr, p. xix.

15. Harper, p. 246.

16. Eleanor Flexnor, *Century of Struggle* (New York: Atheneum, 1973), p. 145.

17. Stanton, p. 255.

18. Katharine Anthony, *Susan B. Anthony: Her Personal History and Her Era* (Garden City, N.Y.: Doubleday, 1954), p. 204.

19. Ibid., p. 205.

20. Ibid., p. 209.

21. Ibid., p. 212.

22. Harper, p. 297.

23. Ibid., p. 298.

24. Anthony, p. 223.

25. Sherr, p. 235.

26. Ibid., p. 236.

Chapter 7

1. Ida Husted Harper, *Life and Work of Susan B. Anthony* (New York: Arno and *The New York Times*, 1969), p. 365.

2. Lynn Sherr, *Failure Is Impossible: Susan B. Anthony in Her Own Words* (New York: Random House, 1995), p. 81.

3. Ibid.

4. Katharine Anthony, *Susan B. Anthony: Her Personal History and Her Era* (Garden City, N.Y.: Doubleday, 1954), p. 257.

5. Patricia G. Holland and Ann D. Gordon, eds., *Papers of Elizabeth Cady Stanton and Susan B. Anthony, Microfilm Edition* (Wilmington, Del.: Scholarly Resources Inc., 1991), reel 15, frames 86–90.

6. Ibid., p. 259.

7. Harper, p. 394.

8. Sherr, p. 208.

9. Ibid.

10. Ibid., p. 249.

11. Mendel, Mesick, Cohen, Waite, Hall Architects, *The Ontario County Court House: Its History and Restoration* (Canandaigua, N.Y., 1988), p. 33.

12. Harper, p. 399.

13. Ibid., p. 473.

14. Ibid.

15. Ibid.

16. Mari Jo Buhle and Paul Buhle, eds., *The Concise History of Woman Suffrage: Selections from the Classic Work of Stanton, Anthony, Gage, and Harper* (Urbana, Ill.: University of Illinois Press, 1978), p. 299.

17. Independence Hall Association, "Liberty Bell," *Historic Philadelphia Homepage*, 1995, p. 1.

18. Buhle and Buhle, p. 303.

19. Elizabeth Cady Stanton, *Eighty Years and More* (New York: Schocken Books, 1971), p. 329.

20. Anthony, p. 355.

Chapter 8

1. Lynn Sherr, *Failure Is Impossible: Susan B. Anthony in Her Own Words* (New York: Random House, 1995), p. 318.

2. Katharine Anthony, *Susan B. Anthony: Her Personal History and Her Era* (Garden City, N.Y.: Doubleday, 1954), p. 382.

3. Ibid., p. 402.

4. Kathleen Barry, *Susan B. Anthony: A Biography of a Singular Feminist* (New York: New York University Press, 1988), p. 308.

5. Sherr, p. 164.

6. Ida Husted Harper, *Life and Work of Susan B. Anthony* (New York: Arno and *The New York Times*, 1969), p. 925.

7. Barry, p. 304.

8. Harper, p. 1113.

9. Ibid.

10. Sherr, p. 27.

11. Ibid., p. 175.

12. Harper, p. 668.

13. Sherr, p. 90.

14. Ibid., p. 308.

15. Ibid., p. 312.

16. Ibid., p. 324.

17. Barry, p. 351.

18. Ibid., p. 354.

Chapter 9

1. Kathleen Barry, *Susan B. Anthony: A Biography of a Singular Feminist* (New York: New York University Press, 1988), p. 355.

2. Ida Husted Harper, *Life and Work of Susan B. Anthony* (New York: Arno and *The New York Times*, 1969), p. 1420.

3. Ibid.

4. Ibid., p. 1391.

5. Ibid., p. 1421.

6. Lynn Sherr, *Failure Is Impossible: Susan B. Anthony in Her Own Words* (New York: Random House, 1995), p. 325.

7. Harper, p. 1437.

8. Sherr, p. 327.

9. Harper, p. 1438.

10. Ibid., p. 1443.

11. Ibid., p. 1444.

12. Sherr, p. 326.

13. Harper, p. 1445.

14. Ibid., p. 1438.

15. Ibid., p. 1410.

16. Congressional Research Service, U.S. Library of Congress, *The Constitution of the United States of America: Analysis and Interpretation* (Washington, D.C.: United States Government Printing Office, 1987) p. 1857.

17. Sherr, p. 328.

18. Lucy Komisar, *The New Feminism* (New York: Franklin Watts, 1971), p. 113.

19. Walter Breen, *Complete Encyclopedia of United States and Colonial Coins* (New York: Doubleday, 1988), p. 471.

20. Sherr, p. 327.

FURTHER READING

Archer, Jules. *Breaking Barriers: The Feminist Revolution from Susan B. Anthony to Margaret Sanger to Betty Friedan*. New York: Viking, 1991.

Kendall, Martha E. *Elizabeth Cady Stanton: Founder of the Women's Rights Movement in America*. Los Gatos, CA: Highland, 1987.

Miller, Douglas T. *Frederick Douglass and the Fight for Freedom*. New York: Facts on File, 1988.

Sherr, Lynn. *Failure Is Imposible: Susan B. Anthony in Her Own Words*. New York: Random House, 1995.

Weisberg, Barbara. *Susan B. Anthony, Woman Suffragist*. New York: Chelsea House, 1988.

For information from the Susan B. Anthony House on the Internet, contact their web site at:

http://www.frontiernet.net/~lhurst/sbahouse/sbahouse.htm

GLOSSARY

abolition—Ending. The nineteenth-century abolition movement demanded an immediate ending of slavery.

abstainer—Someone who does not drink alcohol.

amendment—Addition to the Constitution.

apprentice—To work and learn from an experienced tradesman in exchange for room and board.

coeducation—Males and females studying together in one classroom or school.

Constitution—The agreement signed in 1787 by the founders of the United States that forms the legal basis for American government.

depository—A place for storing documents, typically an office or bank.

Emancipation Proclamation—President Abraham Lincoln's 1863 announcement freeing the slaves in the Southern states.

enfranchise—To gain the right to the franchise, the vote.

feminist—A person who believes in equal rights for men and women.

petition—A request signed by many people that asks for a specific change.

Quaker—A member of the Quaker religion, which is also known as the Society of Friends.

radical—Extreme.

Society of Friends—The Quakers.

suffrage—Right to vote.

temperance—The belief that liquor should not be consumed or sold. In the nineteenth century, strong alcohol such as rum and whiskey were considered "liquor," whereas wine and hard cider generally were not.

universal suffrage—All citizens having the right to vote, regardless of their race or gender.

INDEX